# Turn Vision Into Reality

## From Burnout to Breakthrough

# Chris Moore

### SLP
SOUTHERLAND LANE PUBLISHING

Published by Southland Lane Publishing
Goodlettsville, Tennessee 37072

eBook ISBN: 979-8-9915075-0-9
Paperback ISBN: 979-8-9915075-1-6
Hardback ISBN: 979-8-9915075-2-3
Audiobook ISBN: 979-8-9915075-3-0

# Contents

For my family, Melissa and Bryson.

Melissa, you loved me through my failures and allowed me to further my dream. You are a great mom and make our house a home.

Bryson, God could not have given me a better son. You inspire me to be more and do more.

You both make me want to be a better man and a better dad.

I love you!

\* \* \*

For my parents, Bobby and Nell.

Dad, if I can be half the man that you were, then I will have been success.

Mom, you taught me how to love, care and listen without being judged but by being helped.

Quiet strength, firm correction, and always great love.

# Chapter 1

# From Burnout to Breakthrough

*"Burnout is not a sign of failure. It is a sign that you were trying to give what you do not have."*

Dr, Barbara De Angelis

LOOKING BACK NOW, IT'S clear—I was spiraling into burnout long before I ever realized it. I felt frustrated, overwhelmed, and utterly convinced that I was the only one who knew what needed to be done. But instead of reaching out or communicating, I let that frustration fester, and it grew into something far darker—depression, lethargy, and a deep sense of isolation. It felt like I was sinking, but I had no idea just how deep I'd gone.

It wasn't until that infamous meltdown—my breaking point—that I finally saw the truth. I had been struggling, gasping for air, without even realizing it. That moment was my wake-up call, a stark realization that I was drowning in the very environment I was trying so desperately to control. It wasn't a sudden fall; it was a slow, relentless descent. And it wasn't until I hit rock bottom that I could finally see just how far I had fallen.

It was more than 15 years ago. It was a Tuesday, and I was sitting in my office during our regular weekly manager's meeting. Most of the team was remote, so my sales manager was the only one physically present, and the meeting was not going well. The longer it dragged on, the angrier I got. By the end, only one of my project managers was still on the phone with my sales manager and me. Did I mention things were not going well?

People weren't performing; nothing was going according to the plan I had painstakingly laid out. And I was livid. We were behind on the project, and I blamed these two. Finally, I lost it. I yelled, "This meeting is over," slammed the phone down, and had a few heated words with my sales manager before he angrily stormed out. I was glad he was angry—maybe it would finally motivate him to "get it done!"

As I heard him stomping down the hallway, the thought flashed in my mind: I need to fire him right now. In fact, I need to fire everyone and start over—get rid of these problem children. I stood up from my desk, and just as I heard the door close behind him at the end of the hallway, my phone rang. I pulled out my state-of-the-art Motorola

Razr flip phone, and on the outside notification screen, I saw my wife's name.

I muttered a word I shouldn't have, and in my anger, I threw the phone at the bookcase. As it shattered into pieces, I suddenly stopped, frozen in the moment.

"What is happening to me?"

"Why am I this mad?"

"Why am I letting things get this far out of hand?"

From the outside, everything looked perfect. It seemed like I had it all together. People thought I was living the dream, but the reality was, I was living a nightmare. I spent the rest of the day deflated and quiet, my mind racing.

When I got home, my wife met me at the door and asked how my day had gone. "You know, I've been angry," I said. "I think I've just been extremely angry." She looked at me, puzzled, and asked, "Why are you angry?"

It took me a moment to think.

"I think I decided to be that way," I finally replied.

That realization marked the beginning of my descent into depression. On the outside, everything still looked great, but inside, I was drowning. I couldn't understand what was happening. I had experience, I had gone back to school and earned an MBA—I thought that degree was my golden ticket to business know-how, leadership, and success. And while I'm still proud of that accomplishment, it sure wasn't helping me now.

There was something missing.

This single moment in my life became the catalyst for discovering the missing piece that had been holding me back.

You see, I had spent years studying the lives of the best in business, government, and thought leadership. I had researched over 1,000 CEOs and other great leaders, trying to model their businesses, grasp their concepts, and apply them to my own work. But despite all of this, I was still missing something.

Life just wasn't working for me. I used to look forward to the day, but now... nothing. I tried mindset tricks, morning routines, affirmations, networking, workouts, diets. I implemented new meeting processes, adopted new technology, overhauled the company culture, launched a new logo, rebranded—everything I could possibly duplicate from what I had learned. But none of it solved the burning issue within me. Was I really making a difference? What legacy was I leaving? Did it matter? Did I matter?

Like many others, stress, depression, and anxiety took a severe toll on my health. I ended up flat on my back, overwhelmed. But that overwhelm eventually turned into something else—determination.

## My Go-To Tactic Wasn't Enough

There are a few key moments in each of our lives that change us. I'm not talking about the big ones: injury, death, marriage, or the birth of a child. I'm talking about those moments that guide how we learn from, think about, and react to the events in our lives.

One happened during my sophomore year of high school on the second day of full-contact football practice. This was the first year I ever played. I grew up playing soccer, basketball, and baseball, but sports were different when we moved from Memphis to Nashville. I ended up not playing basketball or soccer; instead, I played football and ran track.

It was just my second day of full-contact football, and I was a little lost. I didn't know anything about football, but since I was a bigger guy, they talked me into playing. It was on that second day that I faced one of the fiercest competitors there's ever been in Tennessee football. (He'll enjoy that I said that.) His name was Lorenzo "Scooter" Edwards. He was a few years younger than me, but physically, he was a man. He was one of the best high school running backs that there's ever been in the state of Tennessee, five foot eight, 180 pounds.

Man could he run! He was solid as a brick, and I definitely felt it on that second day of practice. I was playing defense. Scooter takes the toss from the quarterback and begins to run around the outside edge. Now we had a rule that when the whistle blows, you let up on the guys wearing the yellow jerseys, especially if it was Scooter or our starting quarterback. We definitely did not want to risk injuring one of your best players.

So, as he is coming around the end, here is my opportunity to tackle the best player in Tennessee high school football.

I was just about to him.

He was running full blast towards me.

I was running out towards him-

two more steps...

and the whistle blew...

I let up.

In those last few milliseconds, I saw a smile cross Scooter's face, and he dropped his shoulder and ran right over me as hard as he could.

All I remember is my head spinning to the right and darkness.

I don't know if I was knocked totally out, but I probably was for a couple of seconds. My face mask was planted deeply in the grass and filled the front of my helmet when the sports doctor rolled me over.

I could not quite understand what was happening as they pulled the sod out from in front of my eyes, but the pain told me I was coming back to life. At that point, I saw fingers over my face. He's holding up; what I came to find out was three fingers,

but he holds them up

and I'm looking...

I knew that nine was not the correct answer,

my mind was coming back to me.

So I said three.

Just at that moment, I saw somebody push him out of the way, and I saw this long, angular face looking down at me. He's wearing a worn blue cap with a capital "D" on the front.

He grabs me by the front of my jersey and pulls me up off the ground just a little bit, and he holds up two fingers.

I think I'm about to get the exact same question, but that's not what he said.

*He looked at me and said, "Son, you got two questions to answer. Number one, are you gonna get up? And number two, what are you going to do different so you don't end up down here again?"*

He let go. I fell softly back to the ground.

He stood up, turned around with 2 claps, and said, **"Huddle up. It's time to get back in the game."**

That moment has stuck with me so many times in my life. It's been a guiding beacon.

It's not just the typical thing about getting up, because some people do physically get up. Others, they never get up out of that situation. They are constantly in fear of being there in that spot again. Mentally, they are always knocked down, feeling like they are still lying in the dirt. In that moment, I learned not only about getting up but also about doing something different. I needed to identify what I needed to do to change the outcomes in my life.

This is where my learning started. But there was a third lesson that was holding me back.

A lesson from this moment I did not realize till after my meltdown.

It was a moment of epiphany that gave me a new viewpoint of what I had learned and seen. A new approach that I needed to take. I just had to get a new perspective, and everything began to run in sync.

It was the secret that I was missing.

Coach Ken Redmond was my high school football coach. This was the first of many interactions we would have. He also taught an art class I took during my senior year. Like many others during his 40-year coaching and teaching career, he impacted my life. I see his impact not only in my life but also in the lives and art of my fellow graduates.

It was not just the two powerful questions he asked but how he realized the exact moment I needed to hear that message. He acted. He didn't preach. He didn't scold me. He didn't cuss or try to embarrass me.

He became the man who could step into that moment where I needed a word, provide that word, and then step out of the situation, allowing it to hit me and let it be absorbed within my being. Now, over 35 years later, I continue to share that story and not just share the story but enact it to live it, to take the message and the meaning, and not just affect my life but affect others.

**Those two questions are powerful, but until my meltdown, I didn't recognize the third lesson I should have learned.**

I needed to be him. I became driven to have that level of impact on others, to develop the ability to see and identify that moment when they needed somebody to step in and provide a word, an arm on the shoulder, whatever it was about their situation. They needed someone to step in and offer them a message of hope, a message that provided clarity, a message that provided a way forward that they could not see, or just offer them encouragement that there was a way forward, that there was a way through to the other side of whatever was happening. Not just one of living but one of fulfillment, one of growth. How can I become that person? That became my new endeavor, and it became more than just about reading.

It was about practicing.

It was about participating.

It was about doing.

It was about paying attention and preparing myself for those moments when I could step in and provide that word. Hopefully, in someone's story, 25 or 30 years from now, they will remember me the way I remember Coach Redmond. He passed on a few years ago. Many people came to his visitation and funeral. Men and women that he impacted for years, even decades. He provided that moment for them, just like he did for me.

This realization was the start of a new journey. A new path that took all those strategies and tactics and set them in a new place.

I had to impact people before I could impact outcomes. Authentic leadership and real change do not begin with new strategies, tactics, or actions. It starts with a vision of what is possible and the drive to make that vision a reality.

Coach Redmond had a vision for what he wanted to accomplish. He passed that vision to us in so many ways. He built a culture whose path always pointed to the destination. All his other actions were in support of these two things. If anything was outside these guardrails, it was discarded. Vision and culture were protected at all costs.

Here was the missing piece that put me on the right path.

Thanks, Coach.

# Chapter 2

# Tunnel Vision and ADHD

"Tunnel vision might help you get through the day, but it can keep you from seeing the world."

Unknown

ONCE I STARTED PAYING closer attention to the people and events around me, I realized I was trapped in my own tunnel vision. I was so deeply absorbed in the details of my vision and strategy that I lost sight of whether my team truly understood or engaged with it. In my mind, everything was perfectly mapped out—the destination, the journey, the timelines. I believed I had communicated everything: the vision, our goals, the expectations. Yet, beneath this veneer of clarity and direction, a disconnect was growing.

My vision wasn't as detailed or expansive as it needed to be. It was about me and my business, not about how my team fit into it. I saw them as just another tool. This was a root cause of many of my problems. I often thought I had effectively shared my grand plan, only to discover that my team was adrift in uncertainty. The disconnect came from my failure to fully articulate the 'why' behind our vision, not just the 'what' and the 'how.' The 'why' was about my own reasons, not theirs.

When my team couldn't see themselves as part of the vision or understand their role in it, their commitment and performance inevitably began to wane. They were like actors without a script, uncertain of their lines and the story's arc. Despite the brilliance of my vision, it remained abstract, failing to resonate with those crucial to its realization.

This problem only worsened as I, caught up in my tunnel vision, couldn't understand why the team wasn't performing as expected. I would ask myself, "Why can't they see what's so clear to me?" The answer, however, lay in my own oversight: I hadn't fully defined the vision and strategy in a way that was accessible and meaningful to my team. I didn't micromanage by doing everything myself but by dropping in unexpectedly and disrupting their work with comments that, unintentionally, could be explosive. Even a trivial remark can shatter someone's world when they're not in sync with the overall vision.

Once again, it was my lack of authentic visionary leadership that was the problem. It was me, not my team. No one could thrive in the environment I had created.

Looking back, I often wonder if my actions mimicked the symptoms of ADHD in my team and my business. To an outside observer, it might have seemed like I was constantly jumping from one initiative to another without a clear, cohesive plan. The truth was, I didn't have a concrete grasp on how our immediate actions contributed to the long-term vision I harbored for the business. And I definitely hadn't communicated this to my team, my customers, or my vendors.

The absence of a clear destination or long-term plan created a sense of aimlessness within the team. Even my managers were unaware of the significance of seemingly minor tasks and how they fit into the bigger picture of our long-term success. In pursuing immediate results and quick wins, I overlooked the necessity of a well-defined strategy that aligns short-term actions with our ultimate objectives.

One of the critical areas where this lack of strategic clarity manifested was in our approach to customer acquisition. I wanted a growing customer base but hadn't taken the time to identify and fully define our ideal customers. This lack of specificity not only diluted our marketing efforts but also led us to attract clients who didn't always align with our vision and values.

Additionally, I had allowed our company culture to evolve haphazardly, without intentional shaping or guidance. Without a deliberate cultural strategy, the environment within our organization began to define itself, often in ways that didn't match my vision. This unintentional culture creation led to internal conflicts, miscommunications, and a divergence from the core values I held dear. Different teams developed their own priorities, and an 'us vs. them' mentality began to take root. Internal strife and distrust grew, and blaming others became the norm, with team members referring to each other as 'they' instead of 'we.'

Does any of this sound familiar?

That's right, you've seen it, too.

This phase of my leadership was marked by a paradox: the more I chased various objectives without a coherent plan, the more my team seemed to lose their way. The lack of a clearly articulated strategy and well-defined goals made every new initiative seem disjointed, contributing to a perception of inconsistency and confusion.

The realization hit me hard: this approach was derailing not just specific projects but the very vision I had for the business. To correct course, I had to pause and reevaluate. I needed to comprehensively understand our current position, our desired end state, and the strategic steps required to bridge that gap.

I began to see the need to step out of my tunnel, fully define the vision, and adopt a more inclusive approach. I broke down the grand plan into tangible, relatable details that each team member could connect with. It became crucial for me to share not just the 'what' of our goals but to passionately convey the 'why'—the driving force behind our vision—and how each person fit into that vision.

Additionally, I realized the importance of creating an environment where feedback wasn't just encouraged but valued. This feedback loop acted as a reality check, ensuring our vision remained grounded and aligned with the team's understanding and capabilities. Through this collaborative refinement process, our vision transformed from a solitary dream into a shared mission. In truth, your team will, over time, help to refine and expand your vision in ways you cannot foresee.

Growing in leadership meant recognizing that the clarity of my vision was only as effective as its resonance with my team. It was about understanding that true leadership didn't lie in dictating from the front but in walking alongside my team—guiding, listening, and adapting. Only then could I truly unlock our collective potential, steering our ship toward the desired horizon with everyone on board, fully engaged and passionately committed.

*If you have the right people, doing the right things for the right reasons, headed in the right direction, they will make the right decisions at the right time to execute what you need to accomplish your strategy.*

This is what allows you to achieve your vision.

When you have the right vision and know where you're headed, how you want to get there, and who you want to travel with you, everything becomes much easier.

# Chapter 3

# Why Mission Statements Fail

"People don't buy what you do, they buy why you do it."

Simon Sinek

I HAVE SEEN THE ads and heard the gurus telling you you need a mission statement. They say it is the cornerstone of everything your company will do, guiding your purpose and direction. However, many mission statements fail, leaving employees uninspired, customers disengaged, and business partners puzzled. They need to learn how the mission is supposed to guide them. Where do they fit? What action does it make them take, or should they take?

Here are some examples of company mission statements. If you are in the United States, you probably know the brand, but do you know its mission statement?

1. "We save people money so they can live better."

2. "To provide consumers around the world with delicious, affordable, convenient and complementary foods and beverages from wholesome breakfasts to healthy and fun daytime snacks and beverages to evening treats."

3. "Helping people around the world eat and live better."

4. "To refresh the world in mind, body and spirit. To inspire moments of optimism and happiness through our brands and actions. To create value and make a difference."

5. "To accelerate the world's transition to sustainable energy."

6. "To bring the best user experience to its customers through its innovative hardware, software, and services."

7. "We bring good things to life."

How many of these did you recognize? Based on the mission statement, can you guess their industry and expected outcomes? How many of these could be U.S. Government agencies? (Consumer Product Safety Commission, Department of Agriculture, Department of Energy?) Actually, none are government agencies. You can find the answers at the end of the article.

Mission statements often fail because they don't resonate or connect with people in a meaningful way. While they can be memorized and quoted, they frequently lack the clarity and relevance that make them actionable in daily operations. Employees might understand the mission statement in theory, but without a clear translation into practical, everyday actions, its impact remains superficial. Your mission statement might sound impressive, but if it fails to inspire or guide the day-to-day behaviors and decisions that drive organizational success, it has failed. For a mission statement to be effective, it must be more than a lofty ideal.

There is a scene in the Will Smith movie, Men in Black, that highlights what I am talking about. James Edwards (Will Smith) is invited to an ominous concrete building and is searching for answers. He is brought into a testing room with other recruits. Obviously, everyone is more educated, trained and accomplished that he appears to be, but looks can be deceiving.

My name is Zed," he began, standing stoically in front of the group. "You're all here because you're the best of the best: Marines, Air Force, Navy SEALs, Army Rangers, NYPD." He paused, scanning their faces. "And we're looking for one of you, just one. What will follow is a series of simple tests for motor skills."

A hand shot up, and Zed acknowledged it with an annoying look. "I see we have a question."

"Uh, yeah," James Edwards (Will Smith's character) said, with a smirk. "I'm sorry, maybe you already answered this, but why exactly are we here?"

Another recruit stood up abruptly, snapping to attention.

Zed responded, "Son."

The eager army officer spoke loudly like he was a addressing a Drill Sergeant. "Second Lieutenant Jake Jensen, West Point graduate, with honors. We're here because you're looking for the best of the best of the best, sir!" He looks down at Edwards with disgust, whose response was to start audibly laughing

Zed looked over to see Edwards grinning.

"What's so funny, Edwards?"

Edwards was unable to contain his amusement. "Boy, Captain America over here, the best of the best of the best, sir, with honors." He mimicked the salute, exaggerating the enthusiasm. "You know, he's just really excited, and he has no clue why we're here. That's just, that's very funny to me."

Zed knew he was right, while the other high-valued recruits still had no idea what was really going on.

Like many of our team members, they could recite the mantra but didn't know what it meant. It didn't provide a firm destination or a guide to getting there. So many mission statements are just another version of "best of the best."

Worse yet, the team knows it better than anyone, but they are not the only ones who need to understand it. Our team, customers, vendors, suppliers, and community must also know. They all have a place in its success and a part to play in getting there.

How does a mission statement become and stay relevant for all these groups?

It can't.

When you look at our mission statement examples above, do you think they were created for the enterprise's success or as good marketing copy?

Let's go back to our list of mission statements and discuss number 6: "To bring the best user experience to its customers through its innovative hardware, software, and services."

So who is it?

*Apple.*

Did you get it right?

So, how did this mission statement lead to the iPhone, iPad, Apple Watch, MacBook, and all the different software and ecosystem that Apple offers?

The truth is, it didn't, at least not at first. Steve Jobs had to face massive failure first.

The same lessons that Steve Jobs had to learn are the same concepts that you need to improve your business and your team.

Steve Jobs's ouster from Apple in 1985 was a dramatic turning point in both his career and the company's history. Jobs, who co-founded Apple in 1976, was forced out due to internal conflicts and disagreements with the board and then-CEO John Sculley. Jobs' departure marked the beginning of a turbulent period for Apple, characterized by lackluster product releases, a confused strategy, and declining market share. The company's struggles culminated in the early 1990s, leading to leadership changes and strategic missteps that pushed Apple to the brink of bankruptcy.

In 1996, Apple acquired NeXT, the company Jobs had founded after leaving Apple, bringing him back into the fold. By 1997, he was named interim CEO and, later, permanent CEO. Jobs' return heralded a dramatic turnaround for Apple. One of his first moves was to simplify Apple's product line and focus on innovation, a strategy his "Think Different" campaign introduction underscored.

This campaign wasn't just about marketing but about telling a story that reconnected Apple with its roots of creativity, innovation, and challenging the status quo. Jobs now understood the power of a compelling narrative to inspire employees, excite customers, and reignite the brand's identity.

Jobs' ability to tell a powerful story was instrumental in Apple's resurgence. He framed Apple's mission in a way that resonated deeply with people: Apple wasn't just making computers but empowering individuals to unleash their creativity. This clear, compelling vision helped align the company's efforts and galvanized customer and employee support. The success of products like the iMac, iPod, and eventually the iPhone wasn't just due to their technological innovation but also because each product had a story that connected emotionally with users. The lesson here is profound: a clear and compelling vision-based story can revive a struggling company and transform it into an industry leader.

Apple's mission remained the same, but how the mission's message was crafted and the stories they told changed dramatically.

Steve Jobs' vision for Apple drove its strategy, culture, and, ultimately, execution. Both the internal teams and Apple's customers could see the vision and their place in it.

The vision became the driving force, and the narrative became more significant than a sentence on the wall or at the end of emails.

A detailed vision communicated at all levels to different groups in different ways became the primary driver.

Apple is one of many who discovered that vision comes before mission.

I realize now that my team did not truly understand our vision for the company. Many companies I have worked for and consulted for had the same problem. In some, the mission statement had little to do with the company's overall vision. It was a marketing ploy, a brand statement that some thought would resonate well in marketing campaigns or to gain investment funding. A mission driven by something other than vision is destined for failure.

Another way people lose their way is when the vision is not communicated at every level of the business or is communicated in a way that the vision doesn't seem applicable to that person's role or connected to their daily work. Communicating your vision, your culture, and your core values is the most challenging and most consistently mismanaged part of your responsibilities.

Here are the company mission statement answers.

**Walmart** — "We save people money so they can live better."

**PepsiCo** — "To provide consumers around the world with delicious, affordable, convenient and complementary foods and beverages from wholesome breakfasts to healthy and fun daytime snacks and beverages to evening treats."

**Kraft** — "Helping people around the world eat and live better."

**Coca-Cola** — "To refresh the world in mind, body and spirit. To inspire moments of optimism and happiness through our brands and actions. To create value and make a difference."

**Tesla** — "To accelerate the world's transition to sustainable energy."

**Apple** — "To bring the best user experience to its customers through its innovative hardware, software, and services."

**General Electric** — "We bring good things to life."

# Chapter 4

---

# Vision Before Mission

"Where there is no vision, the people perish..."

Proverbs 19:18 KJV

Y OUR COMPANY'S VISION MUST be the driving force that
controls and guides everything you do. When opportunities
and challenges arise, a simple question—"Does this lead us toward
our vision, or is it taking us off course?"—can make decisions
easier. It becomes simpler to turn down what may seem like a
good opportunity if it doesn't align with your vision. Your vision
is your bedrock. Does this action serve the vision, postpone it, or
derail it?

Many experts refer to the vision as a vision statement, and the text-
book definition goes like this: "A vision statement articulates the
long-term aspirations of a company. It paints a picture of what the
company strives to become or achieve in the future. This aspirational

image isn't confined to the present; it transcends current limitations, inspiring and guiding all stakeholders toward a common goal.

That's fine, but I want you to think of it as more than a single sentence or a brief description like a mission statement. You need a more extended narrative—a story that describes your future state, not just a cliché mantra to be chanted in meetings. Your vision narrative is your origin story, defining your present and future, not just your past.

## Why Vision Matters

Vision provides direction and purpose. It's where everything begins. Simon Sinek's famous "Start with Why" concept is grounded in this very idea. This is where your why begins, and where others will discover why they need to join you.

A vision offers a clear and compelling direction for the future. It serves as a constant reminder of where the company is headed, ensuring that every decision and action aligns with the overarching goal. This directional clarity is crucial for maintaining focus, especially in turbulent times.

Vision is one of our most powerful senses. My grandmother lost her eyesight as she got older. She had to feel the faces of her new grandchildren to know what they looked like and listen closely to their voices. Yet, even after living a long life, the loss of vision made it difficult for her to navigate her own home. She struggled to know exactly where she was, where she was going, and how to get there.

When I was a child, my vision deteriorated dramatically in just a few weeks. Today, I wear contacts or glasses, but without them, I can hardly see anything more than three feet away. My vision is 15/105, plus I have astigmatism. Even if I know you well, I probably won't recognize you if you're standing more than 10 feet away when I'm not wearing my glasses. Yeah, it's bad.

As a kid, I didn't realize how poor my vision was. I had no idea what I was missing. If you've seen videos of people seeing color or hearing for the first time, that was me the day I first put on glasses.

Growing up in Memphis, Tennessee, I remember visiting the eye doctor at Pearl Vision Center. I was in the fourth grade when a Lion's Club group came to our school and told my parents I needed glasses. The eye doctor asked me to read a chart on the wall, but I couldn't even see that there was a chart on the wall. A few days later, we went back to pick up my glasses, and that day, my life changed. I could clearly see the person across from me—I hadn't realized how much I couldn't see.

As we climbed into the car to leave, I was stunned. I could see trees! It was beautiful! I could see the leaves on the trees—each individual leaf. I had never seen that before. To me, a tree was just a green blob. I could hear the leaves rustling but couldn't see them unless they fell on the ground and I picked them up. Everything had been one massive color. I had never seen the streaks of oranges, yellows, and reds in the fall. No, I saw a yellow blob, an orange blob, and a red blob. I couldn't see the beauty around me. But now, everything was crystal clear.

When your vision becomes clear, it opens your eyes to things you didn't see before. As you move closer to your goal, your vision may evolve because you see it more clearly. Vision provides clarity in all aspects of your life, offering more opportunities to focus on the details and reach the destination you've always wanted.

## The Importance of Vision

Without vision, the people perish. And it's not just the people—it's you. As human beings, we are built to look forward. We need hope, aspiration, and something to work toward. Without a vision, we feel like we're going nowhere. Vision is essential in every part of your life, in every category. No matter where you look in your life, you need vision.

Vision also provides direction. It tells us where we're heading and makes it much easier to decide what we will do and how we will get there. Having a distinct vision of exactly where and what we want helps us choose between multiple options. Does option A or option B lead to the vision? Or are they taking us off our path?

Do you know where you're headed? If someone proposes something that doesn't lead toward your vision, it becomes much easier to say no. It's not that it's a bad thing—it could even be a great thing. But does that great thing take you away from your ultimate destination? If it doesn't help you achieve your big vision, saying no becomes necessary to reach your vision.

The truth is, the closer you get to your vision, the clearer it becomes. You may see things you didn't notice before, and your vision may sharpen. The vision becomes even clearer, providing more opportunities. You can better focus on the details to get where you want to go. And as you reach your destination, you may discover new possibilities that were just beyond your horizon. What couldn't be part of your vision yesterday might become part of it tomorrow.

## Inspiration and Motivation

A well-crafted vision statement can inspire and motivate employees, customers, and partners. It acts as a shared source of intrinsic motivation, driving individuals to go above and beyond because they feel part of something greater than themselves.

My dad was a basketball coach when I was growing up. It wasn't his main job, but he volunteered as one of the basketball coaches at the small Christian school I attended. Dad loved basketball. He grew up playing and continued to play as an adult. He also loved to coach.

My school had never had a girls' basketball team until my dad started one. He announced that whoever wanted to play would get to play. Dad made sure everyone had a place on the team, but we didn't have many resources. The only basketballs they had were the larger boys' size. The girls' size balls had been ordered but hadn't arrived. So, Dad asked them to bring a basketball if they had one.

"Just something you can shoot and learn to dribble with."

The girls showed up, excited to be there. Elementary school girls, junior high girls, high school girls—they all came. But Dad discovered something unexpected: many of them didn't even know what a basketball was. They brought volleyballs, soccer balls, and four-square balls. A couple of footballs even made an appearance. I've never seen someone dribble a football.

This was the team Dad started with. It wasn't exactly the kind of team that inspires confidence or dreams of championships. But Dad's vision wasn't just about winning championships. His vision was clear and far more thoughtful than any of us realized.

From the beginning, Dad shared his vision for the program and how this unlikely group fit perfectly into it. He talked about how they would work together, discover their strengths and weaknesses, and capitalize on both. He emphasized the need for heart and commitment to follow the plan. It may not have seemed like he had the right group at first, but his vision was inspiring. The girls were engaged, thoughtful, and practiced hard. They learned the game of basketball, and Dad responded by investing his time, energy, and knowledge into this group of young ladies. In a few short years, they became a formidable force in the girls' basketball league they played in.

My dad passed away a few years ago, but even then, several of these young women reached out—some 40 years later—to remind us how much he had impacted their lives. They spoke of how they knew he cared and how his memory still inspired them.

It's incredible what a shared vision can do. Each player knew they hadn't yet reached the goal, but they understood their part in getting there. They knew where they were headed and were single-mindedly committed to the vision. They believed they could achieve it. Dad defined their expectations: Here's what you need to do, and here's where we're going to end up.

Have you done that for your team?

Are the expectations of your shared vision clearly defined so that everyone on your team shares them? Do they all embrace your core values and culture and know what you expect? These elements create a unified commitment to a shared result. This unity provides stability, which your organization will need. You'll face obstacles, periods of transition, and turmoil. Team members will come and go, and unexpected events will occur. Just think of COVID or the 2008 market crash.

A shared vision helps keep your team together, ensuring they understand what you're all working toward. Individual sacrifices are made for the greater good of the team, especially when they're committed to a shared vision. It also helps identify outliers on your team—those who aren't pulling their weight or don't share your culture. A shared vision helps protect your organization from bad apples you might not have spotted in the hiring process. We all try to avoid hiring people who will undermine our business from within, but we're not always successful. A shared vision helps you and your team identify those individuals, making it clear when someone doesn't align with your culture and vision.

I learned this concept from a businesswoman in Charlotte, NC. She told me their culture was like a wolf pack.

"We are family, and we hunt together. We support one another. We are protective and will defend someone who is part of our pack with our very lives, but the weak need not apply. If someone isn't pulling their load, the pack will let them know. They usually leave on their own. Our culture won't let them stay, but if they don't self-select out of the pack, they will never make it past the first 90-day review."

## Enhancing Execution

We have to see the road ahead to reach our destination. Here's another story about my dad. I miss him, and like most kids, I didn't fully understand what he taught me until I was older—especially now that he's gone. Growing up, guns weren't a big part of our household. My dad didn't enjoy hunting. As a kid, hunting was a chore for him. You hunted for food, and if you didn't bring back a deer, squirrel, or rabbit, you didn't eat. Your family didn't eat. It wasn't a joyful or relaxing time; it was a difficult time. But my dad knew how to shoot. If he could see it, he could hit it.

While we didn't go hunting every year, Dad wanted me to learn how to hunt and shoot. He told me that shooting is all about vision. "If you can see it, just point at it. Your weapon is just like your finger. The gun doesn't even have to be in front of you. It could be close to your holster or out away from your body. If you can see it, you'll hit it, and you'll hit it every time."

Right now, where you're sitting, don't hold your finger out in front of you. Instead, hold your arm out to the side and point your finger at an object. It's an interesting exercise. If you can keep your hand steady, go check, and you'll find your finger is still pointing directly at that object. It's not just the vision of your eye that makes the difference; it's the vision of your mind. When your vision fully connects, reaching your goal becomes second nature, just like pointing your finger.

Our vision becomes our defining focus and guide for everything. It helps define our strategy, brand, culture, and who we need to bring with us on the journey.

## The Role of Mission

A mission statement, on the other hand, defines the company's current purpose and primary objectives. It focuses on the present, outlining what the company does, whom it serves, and how it serves them. While mission statements are crucial for defining the company's purpose, they may lack the aspirational element that inspires different stakeholder groups. They explain what the company does but not necessarily why it does it or where it aims to be in the future. They act as a teaser to draw you into the larger vision narrative. It is the stories we tell that communicate our mission and vision.

Mission statements are often operational and overly focused on the present. They articulate the company's immediate goals and objectives, which may change as market dynamics evolve. Sometimes, they become marketing mantras or just words on the wall, increasingly disconnected from daily activities.

As a company pivots or expands on its journey toward the vision, the mission statement can become outdated or incompatible with current events. We begin to redefine what it means or how it applies. This often happens when the mission statement isn't developed from the vision. If you have a mission statement, go back to the last chapter and consider the four questions. How would you answer them? Is the message congruent? Does it say anything meaningful? Or is it just a variation of "We will be the best at what we do in our market?"

If your company needs help with alignment, engagement, morale, or execution, let your vision guide you.

If you don't believe your vision can accomplish all this, it's because it isn't big or defined enough.

Now, let's explore what goes into designing a vision large and detailed enough to guide you and every other stakeholder to your dream destination.

# Chapter 5

---

# Designing Your Big Vision

"The problems of the world cannot possibly be solved by skeptics or cynics whose horizons are limited by the obvious realities. We need men who can dream of things that never were."

John F. Kennedy

WHEN WE FIRST EMBARK on the journey of building our own business, we all start with a vision—a dream of what the future holds. This vision is often filled with ideas of freedom, success, or simply escaping a frustrating situation. Perhaps it was something you always wanted, or maybe it was thrust upon you by circumstances beyond your control. Whatever your reason, one thing is certain: you had a clear picture in your mind of where you wanted your business to go.

No we're diving into that vision, exploring its power and importance in shaping the future of your enterprise. Because the truth is, vision is where your business begins and ends. It's the cornerstone of everything you'll achieve, guiding your decisions, motivating your team, and serving as the benchmark for your success.

You've probably heard about vision statements from countless business books, webinars, and training sessions. They'll tell you how essential it is to craft a vision statement that encapsulates your company's long-term goals. And while that's a good starting point, it's far from the full picture.

As the leader, your real job is to define, refine, and interpret that vision—over and over again. It's not just about writing a compelling statement; it's about taking that vision and breathing life into it. Your role is to transfer that vision to your team, your customers, and everyone who interacts with your business. So, what does it take to create a compelling vision? How do you craft it in a way that inspires action and drives success?

It starts with where you see your business in the future and the values that will guide you on that journey. Vision isn't just about what you want to achieve in the next quarter or even the next year. It's about looking 10, 15, even 25 years down the road. It's about painting a vivid picture of what success looks like in the long run—without getting bogged down in the tactics of how you'll get there.

Think of it like planning a vacation. When you imagine your dream trip, you don't focus on the hassles of renting a car, airport delays, or lost luggage. You're thinking about the destination—the cruise, the island, Disney World, or the beach. That's the image that drives you to take the trip in the first place.

A compelling vision does the same for your business. It's more than a statement; it's a narrative that embodies your core values and serves as a guiding star for everyone connected to your business.

Start by envisioning the ultimate future of your company. Where do you want to be in 10, 15, or even 25 years? What legacy do you want to leave? How will your company impact the world? What does your business look like at its peak? Who are your customers? What's their experience working with you? What does your team look like, and what kind of culture have you built?

Take the time to write this down. Describe it in detail, but don't get caught up in the how. Focus on the what—what does it look like when you've arrived? Share this vision draft with a trusted colleague, a mentor, or your spouse. Get feedback. Ask, "Does this vision fit me? Does it truly reflect the future I want to create?"

Creating a vision that encapsulates not just where your company is headed, but also aligns with the aspirations of your team, customers, vendors, and suppliers, is no small feat. But a well-crafted vision is vibrant, energetic, and easily understood by all stakeholders. It offers a clear roadmap to a shared future—a future filled with purpose, innovation, and success.

## The Foundation of a Big Vision

A compelling vision goes beyond stating what your company aims to achieve. It embodies your core values and serves as an inspiration for everyone connected to your business. It's not just about setting goals; it's about creating a narrative that's so powerful, it becomes the driving force behind your strategy, culture, and day-to-day operations.

So, how do you craft a vision narrative that works? Start by thinking big—really big. Where do you see your company in the next decade or two? What impact do you want to have on the world? Your vision should be a natural extension of your core values, reflecting the principles that define your company's culture and long-term aspirations.

## Crafting a Vision Narrative

To create a vision that resonates, divide it into sections that address different aspects of your business:

1. **Your Ultimate Success:** Paint a detailed picture of what ultimate success looks like. This is the pinnacle of your achievements—the end goal that drives everything you do.

2. **Your Customers:** Describe your ideal customers. Who are they? What are they like? Where do they live? What attracts them to your business? How will their lives be better because of your products or services?

3. **Your Team:** What does your team look like? How many people are on board? What's it like to work at your company? Describe the culture, environment, and opportunities you want to create for your employees. What perks do they enjoy? How do you ensure they're growing and thriving within your organization?

4. **Your Community:** How do you interact with your community? What role does your business play in making your community a better place? What kind of partnerships and collaborations do you envision?

As you move forward, you can dig deeper into this vision, especially as you share it with your team. Think about the financial aspects—what does revenue growth and profitability look like in this future? What kind of social or community impact do you want to make? What do your operations and facilities look like? What technology are you using? What innovations are you developing? And how does all of this come together to create a company that not only survives but thrives for decades to come?

Integrating Core Values and Culture

Your vision should naturally integrate your core values and demonstrate your desired culture. Here's how to ensure they are woven into the fabric of your vision:

1. **Identify Key Values:** Pinpoint the key values that define your company—integrity, innovation, customer-centricity, sustainability, or whatever else drives your business.

2. **Reflect Values in Vision Statements:** Ensure that each section of your vision reflects these values. For example, if sustainability is a core value, emphasize how your vision prioritizes environmental responsibility.

3. **Communicate Values Consistently:** Consistently communicate these values across all aspects of your business. Your vision narrative should serve as a constant reminder of what your company stands for and strives to achieve.

To ensure your vision is easily understood and energizing, use clear and simple language. Avoid jargon. Be specific and concrete—provide examples that make your vision relatable and tangible for all stakeholders. Infuse your narrative with energy and passion. Your vision should be a source of inspiration, a beacon that excites and motivates everyone involved in your business.

# The Importance of Thoughtfully Designing Your Vision

Taking time to design an ambitious and detailed vision for your company's future is critically important. A well-articulated vision elicits engagement across all levels of an organization by painting a vivid picture of the desired future state. It serves as a guiding light that people can rally behind.

Your vision should stretch people while still being grounded in reality of what you need to accomplish. It should represent big dreams for the future while recognizing current and future constraints. The process of designing a vision requires balancing optimism for what could be with pragmatism about the pitfalls you may encounter along your way.

By investing time upfront to craft your vision, you can create alignment around shared goals and motivate people to take action. A compelling vision provides a unifying roadmap for decision-making at all levels. It becomes more than just words on paper - it's a driving force for progress.

While the vision statement is crucial, the vision must go deeper than just a simple phrase or tagline. To truly come to life, you need to create a robust vision document that fleshes out details and sparks imagination.

Vivid storytelling, concrete examples, and powerful imagery are key tools for breathing life into your vision. By describing what success actually looks like across all areas of your business, you make the future vision tangible. Stories and pictures evoke emotion in a way that dry text alone cannot. The more fully you can render the future state in people's minds, the more compelling your vision will become. A multi-dimensional vision resonates deeply and provides a richer source of inspiration.

## Tailoring Your Vision Message

Your vision must resonate across multiple audiences if it is to gain traction. As such, you need to tailor how the vision is communicated when engaging with different stakeholders.

For investors, emphasize how your vision will drive growth, profitability, and competitive differentiation. Use metrics and market data to convey viability and ambition. For customers, focus on how your vision represents their evolving needs. Paint a picture of how you are innovating now to enable their future desires.

When communicating with employees, underscore how the vision provides meaning and enables progress. Outline specific career development paths in service of the vision. Department heads will key in on execution roadmaps and resource requirements for their areas of responsibility.

So let's go back and start telling me your vision, use stories, make it big, and make it clear. This is going to be your story.

1. What does your business look like? How about your culture? Does your narrative demonstrate your core values, not just list them?

2. Who are your customers? What are they like and what do they like? How will you serve them?

3. What about your team? What are they like? What do they do? Who are they?

4. Tell me about the community you are in and how you interact with them?

Is anything missing? Does it make a good story that you can tell?

Is it so good that when someone hears it, they can't help but tell someone else?

# Chapter 6

# Communicating the Vision

"You can't command commitment; you have to inspire it. One of the best ways to do that is to communicate a clear vision."

James Kouzes

STRATEGY AND TACTICS ARE essential—they keep the wheels turning and help you navigate the challenges of running a business. But they don't create the driving force behind your company's success. That's the role of vision and mission. If you start with the mission, you're already a step behind. The true beginning lies in your vision, and everything else should naturally follow from it.

Let's dig into communication and what it really means. I have a friend who's fond of saying, "Talk is overrated." And honestly, he's onto something. Just talking about something or firing off an email doesn't guarantee true communication. Real communication happens when your message is not just sent but received, understood, and acted upon as you intended. Here's the tricky part: you don't have complete control over how the message is received or interpreted. The complexity of this issue multiplies as your organization grows.

When you're starting out with just a few people, communication is straightforward. You say something, see the results, and make adjustments if needed. Your team can ask questions, observe how you handle situations, and learn directly from you. Building and maintaining a culture in this small environment is relatively simple.

But as your organization expands, communication becomes more challenging. Messages get passed through multiple layers, and like that game of "telephone" we all played in school, they get distorted along the way. By the time your message reaches the frontline, it might be unrecognizable.

The further you are from direct contact with your customers, the harder it becomes to ensure that your vision, mission, and culture remain intact. It only takes one manager interpreting things their way for the whole thing to start unraveling.

## A Lesson from the Frontlines

I remember sitting in a client's waiting room, listening to the front desk staff taking calls. This client took pride in their customer service—responsive, attentive, and highly rated online. They had expanded to three cities in just two years. But if you read the transcripts of the calls I overheard, you'd think two entirely different companies were answering the phone.

One call went like this: "I apologize for your experience this afternoon. We're going to make it right. I've texted one of our supervisors, who's headed to your home now and should be there in about 15 minutes. Please call me anytime if you have more issues. Let me give you my cell number in case I'm not here."

Another call sounded like this: "Look, if you want to set up a service call with one of our technicians, they can answer your questions when they come out. We're pretty busy right now trying to service our customers, and I need to get back to work. The service call will be $75. I can schedule it now, or you can call back when you're ready. Okay, thanks." Click.

After a few minutes, I struck up a conversation with the desk person. They believed customers were only those who paid; everyone else was just "tire kickers" wasting their time. Their performance was measured by customer reviews, documentation accuracy, and how quickly they processed invoices—not by how well they converted leads into appointments. None of the calls were tracked, and the office person wasn't even aware that converting calls was part of their role.

Unfortunately, this attitude wasn't isolated. It had spread throughout the business. A few offhand comments about "tire kickers" and too much focus on "qualifying leads" had infected the staff. The owners, who had an entirely different vision, had two layers of management between them and the frontline staff and were completely unaware of what was happening. When they found out, their initial reaction was anger, but it was misplaced. The real issue was that they hadn't clearly communicated who the customer was and that qualifying leads was a job for marketing and sales—not for the person answering the phone. Their goal was to turn leads into scheduled appointments.

## Alignment at Every Level

This communication gap isn't limited to entry-level or mid-level positions. Your executive and upper management teams need to be just as aligned with your vision and the direction you're heading. If your vision includes multi-state locations, they need to build relationships with vendors who can operate across those states. Your software needs to be scalable, and your payroll and insurance need to cover all your bases—literally.

I once worked with a business owner who expanded to Chicago from Kentucky. They sent some of their Kentucky team to help set up the new location. Unfortunately, one of those employees broke a leg in the Chicago warehouse, and guess what? Their workers' comp didn't cover employees outside Kentucky. The owner had to cover all the medical expenses out of pocket because their insurance agent didn't know about the expansion. Not even their attorney or CPA knew about it. After some work, we restructured their business for better cost savings, insurance policies, and tax structures, but it would have been much easier—and cheaper—if they had communicated their vision from the start.

Getting everyone on the same page with your vision isn't just important—it's essential. But let's be honest: it doesn't happen overnight. It takes time, effort, and a whole lot of communication. And even then, communication is just the starting point. You've got to go further. You need to create feedback loops, set up incentives, and design workflows that make sure everyone is not just hearing the vision but living it.

One of the first things you need to do is regularly check in to see if everyone truly understands the vision and is committed to it. This isn't a one-and-done task—it's something you have to keep at, making sure you're listening for any signs that some folks might be confused or even disconnected. If you notice that a team or department isn't as engaged as they should be, you've got to step in quickly, figure out what's going wrong, and course-correct before things get off track.

It's also important to tie your vision to performance metrics, especially for those in leadership roles. When your leaders are measured on how well they embody and drive the vision, it sends a clear message that the vision isn't just talk—it's a core part of what makes the company successful. And don't forget to recognize and reward those who are really bringing the vision to life. A little recognition can go a long way in reinforcing the importance of alignment.

Creating workflows that cross different departments is another powerful way to make sure the vision is being realized. When teams have to collaborate to achieve the vision, it naturally brings out any areas where people might not be fully aligned. Plus, it builds a sense of shared responsibility, which deepens commitment across the board.

But here's the thing: no matter how well you plan, there will be times when your vision hits a roadblock. Maybe it's an unexpected challenge, or perhaps it's just that the company is evolving in ways you didn't anticipate. When that happens, be ready to tweak and refine the vision. The key is to adapt without losing the core essence of what you're trying to achieve. Flexibility is crucial, but so is staying true to the heart of your vision.

So, in short, aligning everyone around your vision is a dynamic process. It requires clear communication, constant checking in, and a willingness to adapt as needed. But when you get it right, the payoff is huge—a team that's fully on board and working together to turn that vision into reality.

## The Importance of Communicating Your Vision

You've got the vision—it's clear in your head and maybe even written down. But here's the thing: having a vision is only half the battle. The real challenge is making sure everyone else sees it too. That's where communication comes into play. Let's dive into why communicating your vision isn't just important—it's crucial.

Imagine trying to get somewhere without a map or clear directions. You'd end up lost, circling the same block over and over. The same thing happens in a business without a clearly communicated vision. When everyone understands where the company is headed, it's like handing out a map with the destination marked in bright red. Alignment means everyone is on the same page, working towards the same goals, and that's when the magic happens.

Think about it: if your marketing team envisions a world-class brand while your sales team focuses only on short-term wins, you're not going to get very far. Communicating your vision ensures that everyone—whether they're in marketing, sales, HR, or any other department—is moving in the same direction. You want unity of vision, not individual kingdoms working in separate silos.

A vision isn't just a statement; it's a rallying cry. It's the reason your team gets up in the morning and gives their best, day in and day out. When people understand the bigger picture, they're more likely to go the extra mile because they see how their efforts contribute to something meaningful.

A well-communicated vision can turn a regular job into a mission. It's the difference between just selling a product and knowing you're helping to change lives, even in small ways. When your team, customers, and partners feel connected to the vision, their engagement skyrockets. They're not just clocking in and out—they're invested in the journey and excited about the destination, proud of their contribution to the collective dream.

Trust isn't built overnight, but it can be shattered quickly. One of the best ways to build trust is through consistent and transparent communication of your vision. When people know where you're headed and believe in that direction, they're more likely to stick around for the ride. Circumstances may change, tactics may shift, but the vision remains.

Your vision is a promise of the future, and every time you communicate it effectively, you're reinforcing that promise. Over time, this builds a strong foundation of trust and loyalty. Your team trusts that you're leading them in the right direction, your customers trust that you're committed to delivering on your promises, and your partners trust that you're in it for the long haul.

A vision isn't just about dreaming big—it's also about making smart decisions. When you communicate your vision effectively, it becomes a guiding star that helps you navigate the rough waters of life. It's a touchstone that everyone can refer to when making decisions, big or small. Whether you're evaluating a new business opportunity or figuring out how to tackle a challenge, your vision provides the strategic guidance needed to stay on course.

## Strategies for Effective Vision Communication

So, how do you take that vision that's crystal clear in your mind and make sure it resonates with everyone else? It's not enough just to have a vision—you need to make sure it's understood, embraced, and lived by everyone in your organization. Here are some down-to-earth strategies to help make that happen.

## 1. Craft a Vision Statement That Hits Home

Let's start with the basics: your vision statement. This isn't the place for fancy language or corporate jargon. Keep it straightforward, but make it powerful. Your vision statement should be something anyone can grasp and get excited about—whether they're a new hire, a loyal customer, or a key business partner. Think of it as your company's rallying cry.

Consider what made Martin Luther King's "I Have a Dream" speech so unforgettable. It wasn't just the words; it was the vividness, the ambition, the passion. It painted a picture of a future everyone could believe in. Your vision should aim to do the same—clear, compelling, and impossible to ignore.

## 2. Weave Your Vision Into the Company Culture

A vision isn't worth much if it's only talked about at the annual meeting and then forgotten. To make your vision truly stick, you need to weave it into the very fabric of your company culture. This means letting it influence your values, your practices, and even how your team interacts with each other every day.

Think of your vision as something living, breathing, and present in every part of your business. It should be there in the good times and especially in the tough times, guiding decisions and behavior.

## 3. Get the Word Out Through Different Channels

People absorb information in all sorts of ways, so you need to spread your vision using a mix of communication channels. It's not just about sending out an email or mentioning it in a meeting. You've got to use everything at your disposal—team meetings, social media, casual conversations, you name it. The goal is to make sure your message lands, no matter how it's delivered or who's on the receiving end.

## 4. Walk the Talk

As the leader, you're the living, breathing embodiment of your company's vision. Your actions speak louder than words, so everything you do should reflect the vision you're promoting. When your team sees you walking the talk, it reinforces the importance of the vision and inspires them to follow your lead. Remember, people are more likely to follow what you do than what you say.

## 5. Keep the Vision Front and Center

It's easy for a vision to get lost in the day-to-day grind, so don't let it fade into the background. Keep it fresh and top of mind by regularly bringing it up in meetings, during company events, and through other touchpoints. Celebrate the milestones that bring you closer to realizing your vision, and use these moments to remind everyone of the bigger picture. The more you talk about it, the more it becomes a part of your team's daily thinking.

## 6. Share Stories That Bring the Vision to Life

We're all hardwired to connect with stories. They're memorable, relatable, and one of the most powerful ways to communicate. So, use stories to show how your vision is coming to life. Share examples of how the vision has guided decisions, sparked innovation, or led to success. These stories make your vision tangible and help others see it in action.

## 7. Make It a Two-Way Conversation

Your vision shouldn't just be something you hand down from on high. Get your stakeholders—employees, customers, partners—involved in the conversation. Encourage them to share their thoughts, feedback, and ideas. When people feel like they're part of the journey, they're more likely to commit to the vision. This collaborative approach builds a sense of ownership and strengthens the collective effort to make the vision a reality.

By following these strategies, you can ensure that your vision isn't just a statement on paper but a driving force that resonates throughout your entire organization.

## Communicating Vision to Different Stakeholders

Your vision is a powerful tool, but it needs to strike a chord with different groups of people who all have their own perspectives and interests. It's not a one-size-fits-all kind of deal—you have to tailor your message to resonate with each key group. Let's break it down.

### 1. Connecting with Your Team Members

Your team is at the heart of bringing your vision to life, so it's crucial that they get it from day one. When new employees come on board, don't just hand them a handbook and call it a day. Take the time to introduce them to your vision in a way that's meaningful. Make sure they understand how their specific role fits into the bigger picture. This should be a key part of their onboarding process. And it doesn't stop there—reinforce this connection through ongoing training that helps them see their work as part of a larger mission. When they feel like they're contributing to something bigger, they're more likely to be engaged and motivated.

When it comes time for performance reviews, don't just talk about numbers and targets. Use this as an opportunity to discuss how each team member's work aligns with the vision. Celebrate their successes in moving the company closer to its goals and explore ways they can continue to contribute. It's not just about hitting KPIs; it's about making sure everyone is rowing in the same direction.

Regular team meetings are another great way to keep the vision alive. These gatherings shouldn't just be about updates and to-do lists. Use them to discuss progress towards the vision, celebrate milestones, and keep everyone focused on the bigger picture. When the vision is consistently part of the conversation, it stays top of mind for everyone.

## 2. Engaging with the Community

Your vision shouldn't just resonate within your company—it needs to connect with the community as well. Corporate Social Responsibility (CSR) initiatives are a perfect way to align your vision with efforts that benefit the community. Show how these initiatives contribute to both your company's long-term goals and the well-being of the community. Communicate this alignment clearly and consistently through various channels. This makes it clear that your vision isn't just about profit; it's about making a positive impact.

Public relations is another powerful tool for sharing your vision with the broader community. Whether it's through press releases, media interviews, or community events, make sure your vision is always front and center. Highlight your commitment to making a difference and your role in driving meaningful change. When the community sees that your vision extends beyond the bottom line, it builds trust and goodwill.

## 3. Resonating with Customers

Your vision should be the backbone of your marketing and branding efforts. Every piece of advertising, every social media post, and every bit of brand messaging should reflect how your products or services contribute to the vision. This isn't just about selling; it's about connecting with your customers on a deeper level. When they see that your vision aligns with their values and needs, they're more likely to feel a strong connection to your brand.

Customer service plays a huge role in this as well. Train your customer service team to understand and communicate the vision in every interaction. Whether it's a phone call, email, or in-person meeting, every touchpoint should reflect the values and aspirations of your company. When customers feel that your vision is aligned with their needs, it builds lasting relationships that go beyond transactions.

## 4. Collaborating with Vendors and Suppliers

Your vision also needs to resonate with your vendors and suppliers. When you're entering into partnerships, make sure your vision is a key part of the conversation. Incorporate it into agreements and contracts, and ensure that your partners understand and align with your long-term goals. This kind of alignment fosters stronger, more productive relationships that benefit everyone involved.

Regular communication with your vendors and suppliers is also crucial. Keep them in the loop about your progress towards the vision, and discuss how you can work together to achieve mutual success. This ongoing dialogue ensures that everyone is moving in the same direction and that your vision is a shared goal.

By tailoring your communication to these different groups, you ensure that your vision doesn't just stay in your head but truly resonates with everyone who plays a part in making it a reality. It's about creating a shared understanding and commitment that drives your company forward.

## Overcoming Challenges in Vision Communication

Communicating your vision is crucial, but let's face it—sometimes it's easier said than done. Even with the best intentions, you're bound to run into some obstacles along the way. But don't worry; here's how to navigate those bumps in the road and keep your vision on track.

### 1. Keeping Everyone on the Same Page

Consistency is the name of the game. If different leaders or departments start sending out mixed messages about the vision, things can get messy fast. Confusion sets in, and trust begins to erode, which is the last thing you want. The key to avoiding this? Training and resources. Make sure everyone who's communicating the vision—whether it's your top execs or team leads—knows exactly what the vision is and how to talk about it effectively.

This isn't just a one-time deal, either. It's about creating a culture where everyone is aligned and on the same page, day in and day out. Regular refreshers and check-ins can help keep that consistency alive.

## 2. Tackling Skepticism Head-On

Not everyone's going to jump on the vision bandwagon right away, and that's perfectly normal. Some folks might be skeptical, and that's okay. The best way to address skepticism is to be upfront and transparent. Don't shy away from the challenges you're facing or the bumps in the road—acknowledge them. Then, show tangible examples of how the vision is being brought to life and the benefits it's delivering.

When people start to see the vision in action, the skepticism will start to fade. It's all about building confidence through results. Over time, as your team sees that the vision isn't just talk, they'll be more likely to buy in.

## 3. Rolling with the Changes

Let's be real—your company isn't going to stay the same forever, and neither should your vision. As your business grows and evolves, your vision might need a little tweaking too. And when those changes happen, it's critical to communicate them clearly and openly. People need to understand why the change is necessary and how it still aligns with your core values and long-term goals.

Change can be unsettling, but if you explain the reasoning behind it and show how it fits into the bigger picture, you'll help maintain trust and keep everyone moving in the same direction. The key is to adapt smartly without losing sight of what matters most.

By keeping your communication consistent, addressing skepticism directly, and being flexible with change, you can overcome the common challenges that come with sharing your vision. It's all about staying clear, connected, and committed to making that vision a reality.

## Measuring the Impact of Your Vision Communication

It's one thing to share your vision, but how do you know if it's really hitting home? You've got to check in regularly to see if your message is landing where it needs to. This means taking the time to assess how well your vision is being understood and embraced by everyone involved—your team, your partners, and even your customers.

So, how do you do that? Start with some simple tools like surveys, feedback sessions, and performance metrics. These can give you a clear picture of how well your vision is resonating. Are people getting it? Are they on board? Are they inspired to take action? The answers to these questions will help you see what's working and what might need a little tweaking.

Once you've gathered this data, don't just sit on it—use it! Refine your communication strategies based on what you learn. Maybe you need to clarify certain points or use different channels to get your message across. The goal is continuous improvement, so your vision doesn't just stay a statement but becomes a living, breathing part of your organization.

## A Simple Guide to Staying on Track

It's easy for communication to go off the rails, especially when you're juggling multiple messages across different platforms. But there's a simple way to keep things aligned. Before you send out that email, finalize that document, or launch that ad campaign, pause and ask yourself these four questions:

1. Does this represent our vision for the company?

2. What does this say about us and our brand?

3. What does this say about our team?

4. What does this say about our customers?

These questions act like a quick mental checklist to ensure that everything you put out there is aligned with your vision and values. It's a straightforward way to keep your communication focused and on-point.

## The Big Picture

At the end of the day, communicating your vision effectively is what drives alignment, motivation, trust, and strategic direction within your company. It's about more than just words—it's about creating a shared understanding and commitment among everyone involved.

To make this happen, start with a clear and compelling vision statement. Then, embed that vision into your company culture so it's part of the everyday fabric of your business. Use multiple channels to communicate your vision, so it reaches people where they are, in a way that resonates with them.

You'll face challenges along the way—consistency, skepticism, and change are just a few—but by staying vigilant and adaptable, you can overcome these hurdles. Finally, regularly measure the impact of your efforts and be ready to refine your approach as needed. This ongoing process ensures that your vision remains a powerful driving force behind your company's success, keeping everyone aligned and moving forward together.

# Chapter 7

# Who are Your Customers Really?

"People do not buy goods and services. They buy relations, stories, and magic."

Seth Godin

YOU ALREADY DESCRIBED YOUR customers in your vision statement. Here, we are going to go further in your understanding. The deeper your knowledge, the better you can communicate with your team about your customers, define them for your vendors, and deepen your relationships with them.

Your goal is to answer this simple question...

Who are my people?

Your customers don't just live for you and your solutions. They are an entire ecosystem of possibilities. The better you understand that ecosystem, the better you can attract and retain those customers.

After college, one of my first jobs was as a floating assistant manager at Blockbuster Video. This was back in 1996. Mission Impossible and Independence Day were the big hits at the store, but what we got the most calls for was "Six Degrees of Kevin Bacon."

It was amazing who and what he was connected to. The truth is, we are all that way. I know people, who know people, who know people. I'm within 3 degrees of all living presidents from both sides of the aisle. The same could be said for many Grammy-winning artists and Oscar winners. I can also say the same for most business owners in my little town outside of Nashville, my postman, my sanitation worker, and so many others. Relationships become the true currency of life.

What is your relationship with your customer? What do you know about them? Your customers are real people who are more than the simple demographics many use for ad targeting.

The most successful companies across industries all have one thing in common: an intimate understanding of their ideal customer. Leaders like Amazon, Nike, and Salesforce dominate their markets because they are unconditionally dedicated to knowing and serving their customers.

Knowing your customer is invaluable for multiple reasons:

**Laser-Focused Marketing:** When you understand your ICP thoroughly, your marketing team can create highly targeted campaigns that speak directly to their needs and preferences. This increases engagement and return on marketing investment.

**Higher Lead Conversion:** With an ICP, your sales team is equipped to better identify and qualify leads, improving conversion rates and reducing cycle times.

**Optimized Product Development:** Knowing your ICP means your product team can consistently prioritize and deliver features that align with real customer needs.

**Improved Customer Experience:** Every customer touchpoint can be optimized - from purchasing and onboarding to product usage and support - when you design with your ICP as the guiding light.

**Enhanced Loyalty and Advocacy:** Customers who feel truly understood are more satisfied and likelier to stick with you long-term and refer others.

The benefits range from top-line revenue growth to higher customer lifetime value. Constructing it requires dedication, research, and insight from stakeholders across your company. It is a continuous process, demanding openness to revising your assumptions as you gather more data and your business evolves.

In this chapter, we will learn how to find our perfect customers. You will know who your customers are and who they are not. We will also learn how the process differs for business-to-consumer (B2C) versus business-to-business (B2B) organizations.

Overall, you need to consider the ecosystem in which they exist. Where do they live, and how do they live? Who exactly are your people?

By the end of this chapter, you will know how and when to use three customer profiles.

1. The Ideal Customer Avatar (ICA)

2. The Ideal Customer Profile (ICP)

3. The Buyer Persona

## Business to Consumer: How to Define Your Ideal Customer Avatar

Long-term business success is all about really knowing who your customers are. And this isn't just important—it's essential, especially if you're in the game of selling directly to consumers. Whether you're aiming to make your product or service go viral or capture the lion's share of the market, understanding your customer is the key to success.

But here's the thing: knowing your customer isn't just about demographics or market segments. It's about digging deeper—building a complete picture of the person whose needs and desires align perfectly with what your business offers. That's where the Ideal Customer Avatar (ICA) comes in.

Crafting your ICA isn't just another marketing exercise; it's the foundation of a targeted business strategy that can drive growth and boost profitability. When you really nail down your customer avatar, you can personalize your approach and create a connection that truly resonates with your audience.

Now, the term "Ideal Customer Avatar" might sound like another business buzzword, but it's far more than that. It's a powerful strategic tool that can help you increase profits and reduce headaches. So, what exactly is an ICA? It's a detailed, semi-fictional profile that represents your perfect target customer. This profile gives you a 360-degree view of your customer's demographics, interests, values, pain points, and behaviors.

In short, an ICA encapsulates all the insight you need to ensure your brand not only resonates with your audience but also converts them into loyal customers. It's about understanding your customers so well that your business becomes the obvious choice for them.

The impact of having an Ideal Customer Avatar (ICA) is huge—it touches just about every part of your business.

When it comes to marketing, knowing your ICA means you can create campaigns that speak directly to the issues, interests, and media habits of your ideal customer. Instead of casting a wide net and hoping for the best, you're sending a message that's laser-focused on what matters most to them.

For product development, your ICA ensures you're consistently addressing the real needs and motivations of your customers. You're not just creating products for the sake of it; you're making things that truly resonate with your ideal customer and solve their problems.

Your content strategy? With an ICA in place, you can design content that provides real value at every stage of the purchasing journey. Whether your customer is just discovering your brand or ready to make a purchase, your content will meet them where they are and guide them to the next step.

Even customer support benefits from a well-crafted ICA. By understanding the preferences and expectations of your ideal customer, your support team can deliver an experience that feels personalized and attentive. It's about making every interaction count.

In short, the ICA turns a broad target audience into a clear, actionable profile that guides your strategy. And this isn't just theory—cross-industry studies show that companies with accurate ICAs have seen a 20% increase in conversion rates, doubled the effectiveness of their ad spending, and boosted customer lifetime value by 38%.

The power of the ICA lies in its ability to bring specificity and personalization to every part of your business. It's not just a tool; it's a growth engine that can drive real, measurable results across the board.

> *If I asked you to describe your perfect customer right now. What would you say?*
> *Do you know precisely how to briefly describe them and be able to name 5 people that fit the profile?*

Creating your Ideal Customer Avatar (ICA) is more than just a quick exercise—it's about diving deep into the attributes, needs, aspirations, and challenges of the person who would most benefit from what you're offering. When you take the time to really understand this person, you're setting your business up to craft marketing strategies that hit the mark, develop products that genuinely meet your customers' needs, and deliver messages that resonate on a personal level.

Think about it this way: the businesses that truly get their customers—who know them almost as well as they know themselves—are the ones that see higher conversion rates, greater customer satisfaction, and stronger financial results. On the flip side, those that don't invest in this understanding often struggle to connect, and it shows in their bottom line.

The real game-changers, the pioneering companies, use their ICAs as a guiding light for everything they do. Whether it's product development, customer experience, content creation, or any other touchpoint along the customer journey, they make sure everything is aligned with their ICA. This approach ensures that their messaging and offerings are consistent and resonate deeply with their target audience.

In this section, we're going to explore just how transformative it can be to really know your ICA. We'll break down the steps you can take to define this critical profile for your business and show you how it can lead to more focused strategies, better products, and a loyal customer base that keeps coming back.

### *Give Your Avatar a Name.*

Something powerful happens when you give your Ideal Customer Avatar a name. Suddenly, they're not just a theoretical concept or a set of statistics—they become a person with a human essence. This simple act of naming turns your avatar from a vague idea into someone relatable, someone your team can actually picture and connect with.

Think about it: when you start talking about "Emily, the tech-savvy millennial mother," instead of just saying "female, age 25-34, with an interest in technology," the conversation shifts. It's no longer abstract; it becomes personal. Your marketing team can imagine Emily's day-to-day life, her challenges, and her needs. They can think about what would really catch her attention or make her life easier. Discussions about marketing strategies, product development, and customer service take on a whole new dimension because now, you're not just trying to appeal to a faceless demographic—you're trying to connect with Emily.

This shift makes your messaging more tailored and meaningful. When your team is focused on pleasing and understanding "Emily," their decisions naturally become more personalized. Campaigns become more targeted because they're crafted with Emily in mind, seeing the world through her eyes. This kind of specificity can lead to marketing that resonates on a deeper, more personal level with your audience.

Naming your customer avatar also grounds your strategies in reality. It fosters empathy within your team and provides a clear direction for your brand's voice, tone, and overall strategy. There's research to back this up, too. A study by Facebook IQ found that giving avatars human names increased purchase intent by up to 30% compared to using generic labels like "suburban moms." And that's not all—other studies have shown clickthrough rates can be as much as 47% higher when personalized names are used in ad copy. It's proof that focusing on the individual can help you reach a wider audience.

Another benefit of naming your avatar is how it changes the way you ask questions. Instead of wondering, "What would our target demographic think about this?" your team can ask, "How would Emily feel about this?" This shift encourages more customer-centric thinking, leading to decisions and innovations that are squarely focused on the customer.

In short, naming your Ideal Customer Avatar isn't just a small detail—it's a game-changer. It helps your team build stronger emotional connections, fosters more personalized strategies, and ultimately drives better results. When you focus on the individual, you make your brand more relatable, more impactful, and more successful.

***If you want to know your customer, you have to really know your customer.***

It's not enough to just scratch the surface—you need to dig deep and build a comprehensive record of who they are and what their world looks like. This record should become the lens through which every business decision is made, whether you're launching a new product or crafting your next marketing campaign.

As you start integrating this understanding into your daily operations, you'll notice something remarkable: your approach to everything becomes more cohesive and aligned. Every move you make will be aimed at pleasing "Emily" or whatever name you've given your customer avatar. And here's the thing—if an idea or strategy doesn't align with what would make Emily happy, you'd better have a compelling reason to move forward with it anyway.

Now, let's talk about something else you need to consider.

## You Probably Have More Than One Ideal Customer Avatar.

Here's a simple truth: most businesses have more than one ideal customer avatar. I know this might sound like it goes against what some other business gurus say, but it's the reality. Think about a used car dealer, for example. They might have one customer avatar that's a family with four kids, trying to help their oldest buy their first car. At the same time, they might have another avatar—a middle-aged single person looking to replace an aging vehicle. Both avatars may share a common trait, like having a lower disposable income, but their motivations and expectations are entirely different.

The same principle applies to your business. Especially if you're looking to break into new markets, you'll find that you have more than one type of customer you need to consider. Now, I wouldn't go overboard—two or three profiles should be your maximum. But it's crucial to ensure that any advertising promotion or organizational change doesn't negatively impact another primary market segment you're targeting.

We'll dive deeper into market segmentation later in this chapter, but for now, just remember this: understanding your different customer avatars allows you to tailor your strategies in a way that speaks directly to each segment, ensuring that you're meeting the diverse needs of your entire customer base.

## Who Do You Not Serve?

"Focus on who you serve; others will benefit from knowing exactly who you don't serve." – Laura Kelly

When you're crafting your perfect customer avatar, it's just as important to think about who you don't want to serve. Knowing who isn't the right fit for your business can be just as powerful as knowing who is. It helps streamline your customer targeting by steering away leads that are unlikely to convert or stick around. These are the customers who might end up causing more headaches than they're worth, draining resources from sales to distribution.

Let's break it down with a few examples:

- *"Our customers don't haggle over price. They're looking for a quality product that lasts. If someone's after something fast and cheap, we're not the right fit."*

- *"We respect our customers, and we expect the same in return. We don't do drama—if a customer brings that, we're happy to show them the door."*

- *"Our restaurant is loud and fun. If someone's looking for a quiet place to chat, this isn't it."*

You can be as specific as you like with these statements. Sure, in today's culture, there's a fine line to walk when it comes to being selective, but it's necessary to be clear about who you're serving. Take a high-end restaurant, for example. If your cheapest meal is $120 a person, it's not practical to spend advertising dollars trying to attract a single mother of three working two jobs to make ends meet. That's an extreme example, but it illustrates the point: knowing who isn't your customer helps you focus your resources where they'll have the most impact.

This clarity doesn't just help your marketing—it helps your whole team and even your vendors understand your business better and align with its direction. By knowing who you don't serve, you keep your focus sharp on your Ideal Customer Avatar.

This is especially crucial in the Business-to-Business (B2B) world. If part of your strategy involves selling to other businesses, you need to approach it a bit differently than you would with an Ideal Customer Avatar. In B2B, being clear about who isn't the right fit is vital for maintaining strong, mutually beneficial relationships with your business clients.

In short, defining who isn't your customer is a key part of staying focused on who is. It's about making sure your efforts, from marketing to customer service, are aligned with serving those who truly benefit from what you offer, while avoiding those who might not be the right match.

## Business-to-Business Customers

While many of the concepts and questions from the Ideal Customer Avatar (ICA) exercise still apply, approaching a business customer requires a different strategy. For instance, while "Emily" might be the perfect end-user of your product, she might not be your ideal contact in a business-to-business (B2B) setting. When it comes to B2B, there's a lot more to consider.

Not all methods of targeting business customers are created equal. Two key frameworks stand out when it comes to capturing business market share: the Ideal Customer Profile (ICP) and the Buyer Persona. These terms might sound like they're interchangeable, but they serve different purposes in the world of marketing. You might even think they're just another version of the ICA, especially when it comes to the Buyer Persona, but that's not the case. The motivations and goals of a business customer are distinct from those of an individual consumer.

In this context, the Ideal Customer Profile (ICP) focuses on identifying the types of businesses that are the best fit for your products or services. It's about understanding the characteristics of companies that are most likely to benefit from what you offer and, in turn, drive your success. This could include factors like company size, industry, revenue, and geographic location. The ICP helps you zero in on the businesses that have the potential to be long-term, profitable clients.

On the other hand, the Buyer Persona delves deeper into the specific individuals within those target businesses who make the purchasing decisions. These are the people who will actually interact with your sales team, evaluate your product, and decide whether or not to buy. The Buyer Persona focuses on understanding their roles, responsibilities, pain points, and what drives their decision-making process.

While these two frameworks are different, they work hand in hand to help you build a comprehensive B2B strategy. The ICP helps you identify the right businesses to target, and the Buyer Persona helps you understand how to engage with the decision-makers within those businesses effectively.

In the next section, we'll break down the differences between the ICP and the Buyer Persona even further and explore how they complement each other. Together, these tools will help you define not just the businesses but also the key players who will move you toward your goals.

## Understanding the Ideal Customer Profile (ICP)

Let's start by getting clear on what an Ideal Customer Profile (ICP) really is. Think of the ICP as a detailed model of the perfect company—not an individual—that would gain the most from your product or service. It's like a blueprint that guides your sales and marketing teams to focus on the leads that are most likely to turn into high-value customers. Targeting the wrong businesses isn't just a waste of time; it can seriously hurt your profitability. That's why crafting an ICP is so crucial.

An ICP involves creating a comprehensive archetype that includes details like the company's size, industry, financial health, location, online behavior, and even their current client base. But this isn't just a surface-level sketch—it's a deep dive into the core characteristics of companies that are not only likely to buy from you but also stay loyal and become strong advocates for your brand.

When you focus on clients that fit this profile, your marketing efforts become laser-focused, which can lead to significant savings on advertising costs and a much better return on investment (ROI). Think of the ICP as a "lead filtration system." It ensures that your business is spending its time and resources on engaging with companies that have the highest potential for long-term partnerships and profitability.

Whether you're a startup or an established company, tailoring your product features, customer support, and sales initiatives to match your ICP can be a game-changer. It can trigger significant growth and help you dominate your market.

Let's break it down with a few examples. Some businesses specialize in helping distressed companies with loans or investment capital. Others target blue-chip companies with solid financials. If you make high-end audio equipment for cars, you'll probably want to focus on aftermarket companies or custom car shops, not commercial truck manufacturers. Similarly, a small business with just 5-10 employees might not have the budget for your services. The ICP helps you identify the right prospects and aligns your efforts with your market goals.

Creating an ICP isn't just a smart strategy—it's a revenue-generating engine. By aligning your marketing and sales efforts with your ICP, you're setting yourself up for more focused lead generation where quality beats quantity every time. When you target companies that are a great fit for your offerings, you're more likely to close deals at a higher conversion rate, which has a direct impact on your bottom line.

One of the biggest advantages of using an ICP approach is that it allows you to spend your advertising budget wisely. Instead of casting a wide net and hoping something sticks, your ICP lets you target specific segments that are much more likely to convert. This means you get a better return on your ad spend (ROAS) and more bang for your buck.

Precision marketing like this also helps streamline your sales cycle. When you're going after the right leads, the sales process tends to move faster because there are fewer objections and a clearer need for what you're offering. Your product development team benefits too. A well-defined ICP helps them align product features, user experience, and customer service more closely with what your best customers actually need. This kind of alignment fosters innovation and ensures that your products are a perfect fit for the market.

Lastly, businesses that successfully integrate ICPs into their operations often see a boost in their Net Promoter Score (NPS). Why? Because when customers feel understood and well-served, they're more likely to become promoters. They'll naturally recommend your product or service to others, which expands your reach and amplifies your impact. A higher NPS means stronger customer loyalty, lower churn rates, and a higher customer lifetime value (CLTV), all of which contribute to a significant surge in your revenue.

In summary, developing and implementing an ICP isn't just a strategic move—it's a smart, revenue-boosting approach that can transform your business by helping you target the right companies, streamline your processes, and foster stronger, more loyal customer relationships.

Once you know your ICP, you need to define your Buyer Persona.

## The Buyer Persona

The Buyer Persona isn't the same thing as your Ideal Customer Avatar (ICA). Earlier, we talked about Emily as the ICA—a representation of your ideal end consumer. But when you're dealing with a business, the person making the buying decisions isn't Emily; it's someone entirely different. Let's say her name is Natalie. Natalie is your Buyer Persona, and she's got a whole different set of concerns and priorities compared to Emily.

Emily, the consumer, might only care about how well the product works for her needs. She's focused on the features, the benefits, and how it fits into her life. But Natalie, who's working at the business you're targeting, has a lot more on her plate. She's thinking about wholesale margins, payment terms, delivery timelines, quantity requirements, returns, warranties, and a dozen other factors that Emily wouldn't even consider. Natalie might also be just the gatekeeper—the person you need to win over before you can even get to the final decision-maker in the company.

So, the way you approach and sell to Emily versus Natalie needs to be different if you want to be successful. Understanding the distinction between an Ideal Customer Profile (ICP) and a Buyer Persona is crucial for tailoring your outreach and communication strategies.

Your ICP is all about the ideal business—the type of company that would get the most value from your product or service. It helps you identify which doors your sales team should be knocking on. But once you're in the door, the Buyer Persona comes into play. The Buyer Persona is a detailed, semi-fictional representation of the individual within that company who will be making the purchasing decisions. This persona is enriched with specifics like demographics, job titles, personal aspirations, and even lifestyle choices. It's about understanding who they are as a person so you can connect with them on a human level.

Buyer Personas help to humanize the marketing process. They make it easier to craft personalized communication and more empathetic interactions with potential customers. These personas are incredibly useful across all departments—sales, marketing, content creation, and even product design—because they allow for a tailored approach to each individual rather than relying on a one-size-fits-all, mass-market strategy.

One of the biggest misunderstandings is thinking that the ICP and the Buyer Persona are interchangeable. They're not. The ICP tells you which companies are worth your time, but the Buyer Persona tells you how to talk to the people within those companies. Both are essential for a well-rounded marketing strategy, but they serve distinctly different purposes. When you use them together, you're not only ensuring that you're targeting the right companies, but you're also making sure your message resonates with the individuals who have the power to make decisions.

In short, mastering both the ICP and the Buyer Persona means you'll be talking to the right people in the right way, increasing your chances of turning leads into sales and building long-term business relationships.

## Market Segments: You May Have More than One

Just like with your Ideal Customer Avatar (ICA), you might find that your business has multiple ideal clients. This is where market segmentation comes into play. Market segmentation is all about breaking down a broad market—whether it's consumer or business—into smaller groups, or segments, based on shared characteristics. These characteristics could be anything from company size and revenue to the technologies they use or the values they uphold.

To get started, think about the different types of companies that would benefit most from your product. For example, if you're a SaaS company, your ideal segments might include emerging tech companies, businesses looking to streamline operations, or organizations that lack a specific software capability that you provide. On the other hand, if you're in the fintech space, you might focus on companies that need help with operational efficiency, financial data analytics, or risk management solutions.

Once you've identified these broader segments, it's time to get specific. Narrow down and identify the top companies within those segments. Define these ideal companies using criteria that align closely with your product or service. This could include factors like the number of employees, annual revenue, the technologies they currently use, geographic location, or even their organizational values and culture, especially if they align with your own.

It's also useful to contrast your ideal customer profile with an "anti-ideal" profile. By clearly understanding the types of customers you don't want, you can more accurately target those who will genuinely benefit from what you offer. This approach helps you qualify prospects more effectively, saving time and energy that would otherwise be spent chasing leads unlikely to convert or be satisfied in the long run. Knowing who not to target allows your marketing team to focus their efforts where they'll have the most impact.

Don't underestimate the power of a well-defined customer profile. This framework doesn't just sit on paper; it influences almost every aspect of your business, from sales strategies to customer satisfaction. When you focus on a clear market segment, you're optimizing for both profitability and efficiency. Your marketing team will be able to craft highly targeted campaigns, your sales team will become more skilled at qualifying leads, and your product development team can tailor features to meet the exact needs of your ideal customers.

Incorporating the ICP methodology into your customer targeting strategy should go hand in hand with creating tailored content and messaging. This ensures that your marketing materials speak directly to the challenges and aspirations of the companies you're trying to reach. Additionally, train your sales team to recognize these ideal customers, engage with them effectively, and speak their language. This will enhance their ability to form meaningful connections and close deals more efficiently.

It's also important to measure the impact of your ICP strategy. Set clear benchmarks and key performance indicators (KPIs) to gauge whether your targeting efforts are delivering the expected results. Be ready to adjust and improve your ICP strategy as you gain more insights and as the market evolves. Remember, while the ICP framework is powerful, it works best when combined with other strategies like developing detailed Buyer Personas, leveraging data analytics, and continuously listening to customer feedback. It's the combination of these elements that leads to sustained growth and success.

So, as you build and refine your ICP, keep in mind that it's not just about identifying the right companies—it's about creating a holistic strategy that aligns every part of your business toward attracting and serving those companies effectively.

Below is a guide to help you develop your Ideal Business Customer Profile and Buyer Persona.

# B2B Ideal Customer Profile (ICP) Development Guide

## Industry Characteristics

**Industry Sector:** What industry or industries does your ideal customer operate in?

**Market Size and Growth:** How large is the industry? Is it growing, stable, or declining?

**Regulatory Environment:** Are there specific regulations that impact these businesses?

## Company Characteristics

**Company Size:** What is the company's size in terms of revenue and number of employees?

**Geographical Location:** Where are these companies located? Are they local, national, or international?

**Type of Business:** Are they B2B, B2C, non-profit, government, etc.?

## Financial Health

**Revenue:** What is the typical annual revenue range?

**Profitability:** Are these businesses typically profitable and financially stable?

**Funding Status:** Are they self-funded, venture-backed, publicly traded, etc.?

## Operational Characteristics

**Technology Adoption:** Are they early adopters of technology or late adopters?

**Business Model:** What business model do they operate (e.g., subscription, service-based)?

**Purchasing Process:** What does their purchasing process look like? Who is involved in the decision-making?

## Pain Points and Needs

**Challenges:** What are the primary challenges or problems they face that your product/service can solve?

**Goals:** What are their short-term and long-term business objectives?

**Current Solutions:** What solutions are they using, and what are their gaps?

## Decision-Maker Characteristics

**Roles and Titles:** Who are the decision-makers or influencers in the purchasing process?

**Professional Backgrounds:** What is their typical professional experience and background?

**Personal Drivers:** What motivates them professionally? (e.g., cost-saving, efficiency, innovation)

## Cultural Fit

**Company Culture:** What type of company culture do they have (e.g., innovative, conservative)?

**Values and Ethics:** What are their core values and business ethics?

**Social Responsibility:** Do they prioritize social responsibility and sustainability?

## Relationship to Your Product/Service

**Awareness:** Are they already aware of your product/service?

**Perceived Value:** How might they perceive the value of your offering?

**Potential Objections:** What objections might they have to using your product/service?

*Instructions for Use:*

*Research and Data Collection: Gather data from market research, existing customer data, sales team input, and industry reports.*

*Collaborative Approach: Involve team members from sales, marketing, product development, and customer service.*

*Iterative Process: Regularly review and update the ICP as you gain more insights and as market conditions evolve.*

*Application: Use the completed ICP to guide marketing strategies, sales approaches, product development, and customer service initiatives.*

# B2B Buyer Persona Development Guide

## Demographic Information

**Title and Role:** What is the job title and role within the organization?

**Age Range:** What is the typical age range of the decision-maker?

**Education Level:** What level of education do they typically have?

## Professional Background

**Career Path:** What common career paths or previous roles have they held?

**Skills and Expertise:** What specific skills or areas of expertise do they have?

**Professional Goals:** What are their main professional objectives and career aspirations?

## Company Role

**Decision-Making Authority:** What level of decision-making authority do they hold?

**Role in Purchasing Process:** Are they a primary decision-maker, influencer, or end-user?

**Internal Influence:** How do they influence others within their organization?

## Challenges and Pain Points

**Primary Challenges:** What are the main challenges they face in their role?

**Needs and Desires:** What are they actively seeking solutions for?

**Frustrations with Current Solutions:** What are their frustrations with current products/services in the market?

## Motivations and Drivers

**Personal Motivators:** What personally drives them in their professional decisions (e.g., recognition, achievement)?

**Business Drivers:** What business outcomes are they aiming to achieve (e.g., cost reduction, efficiency)?

## Media and Information Consumption

**Preferred Information Sources:** Where do they typically gather information or news (e.g., industry publications, social media)?

**Influencers and Thought Leaders:** Who do they admire or follow in their industry?

**Learning Preferences:** How do they prefer to learn about new products or services (e.g., webinars, whitepapers)?

## Communication Preferences

**Communication Style:** What is their preferred style of communication (e.g., direct, detailed)?

**Preferred Channels:** How do they prefer to be contacted (e.g., email, phone, in-person meetings)?

## Objections and Concerns

**Potential Objections:** What objections might they have regarding your product/service?

**Risk Considerations:** What risks or concerns do they consider when making decisions?

*Instructions for Use:*

*Gather Insights: Utilize interviews, surveys, sales feedback, and customer interactions to gather information.*

*Team Involvement: Encourage collaboration from various departments (sales, marketing, customer service) for diverse perspectives.*

*Persona Validation: Validate the Persona with real customers and update it based on feedback.*

*Application: Use the Persona to tailor marketing messages, sales pitches, and product development to your target decision-makers specific needs and preferences.*

Adopting an Ideal Customer Profile and Buyer Persona is not a one-off event but a continuing process that requires informed decision-making and company-wide adoption. To seamlessly incorporate this approach into your business, start by gathering data. Utilize every touchpoint - sales data, customer feedback, social media insights, etc. - to create a multi-dimensional view of who your ideal customer really is. Collaborative input from sales, marketing, customer success, and even product development roles is crucial for painting an accurate picture. Once the data paints a clear image, formalize your ICP document. This should be a living document, regularly revisited and honed as your market environment evolves and your business grows. A detailed ICP should be easily accessible to all stakeholders in the company, ensuring alignment and uniformity in targeting the right prospects.

As we come to the end of this exercise, let's reiterate the significance of deeply understanding your customer base, be it in a B2C or B2B context. The construction of the Ideal Customer Avatar, Ideal Customer Profile, and Buyer Persona is a strategic tool that shapes the trajectory of your business. By identifying your 'Emilys' and 'Natalies,' you create a lens through which all business decisions can be evaluated for relevance and impact.

As the market evolves, the ability to adapt and refine these profiles is as crucial as their initial creation. The landscape in which your customers operate will change, influenced by technological advancements, economic shifts, and cultural trends. Staying tuned into these changes and reflecting them in your customer profiles ensures that your business remains relevant and responsive.

Remember, knowing your customer demands constant dialogue with your market, a keen eye on emerging trends, and a willingness to question and refine your assumptions. As you progress, you'll find that this deep understanding of your customers drives sales and marketing efficiency, fosters innovation and customer loyalty, and heightens brand recognition.

Knowing your customer is a cornerstone of your business strategy, driving growth, innovation, and long-term success. So, let's move forward focused on the people who make our businesses thrive: our customers.

# Chapter 8

---

# Designing Your Strategy

"Vision is a destination – a fixed point to which we focus all effort. Strategy is a route – an adaptable path to get us where we want to go."

Simon Sinek

AT ITS CORE, STRATEGY is about big-picture planning. It's the process of setting long-term goals and figuring out the best way to reach them, especially when the future is uncertain. Think of strategy as the map that shows you where you want to go and the roads you need to take to get there. It's not just about choosing the right path—it's also about knowing which paths to steer clear of. Strategy provides direction and purpose to everything an organization does.

On the other hand, tactics are the specific actions or steps you take to execute that strategy. If strategy answers the "what" and "why," tactics answer the "how." They're the practical moves you make to bring the strategic plan to life.

These concepts—strategy and tactics—are fundamental in business, the military, and countless other fields. However, they're often confused or used interchangeably, leading to a lot of misunderstandings. When people mix up strategy and tactics, they can lose sight of the bigger picture, which is crucial for long-term success.

Let's break down the differences a bit more. Strategy is broad in scope. It's like the master plan that guides an entire organization or a major initiative. It encompasses many different activities and decisions, shaping the overall course of action. Tactics, by contrast, are much narrower in focus. They deal with the immediate steps you take to execute the strategy and respond to current situations.

Timeframes also set strategy and tactics apart. Strategic planning is about the long haul—it's thinking years, even decades ahead. It's about envisioning where you want to be in the future and charting a course to get there. Tactical planning, however, is all about the here and now. It's focused on short-term actions and quick responses to changing circumstances.

Another difference is in how fixed or flexible they are. Strategy tends to be more stable. It doesn't change unless there's a significant shift in your environment or goals. Tactics, on the other hand, are more dynamic. They can and should be adjusted quickly to meet immediate challenges or seize opportunities, giving them more flexibility than the overarching strategy.

Who makes these decisions also varies. Strategic decisions are typically made by top-level management or leaders who have a broad view of the organization and its surroundings. They need to consider a wide range of factors, from market trends to competition to the company's internal strengths and weaknesses. Tactical decisions, however, are often made by mid-level or lower-level managers. These folks are closer to the day-to-day operations and have a detailed understanding of the tasks at hand.

In the business world, for example, a company's strategy might be to dominate a specific market segment. The tactics to achieve this could include launching targeted marketing campaigns, developing innovative products, or forming strategic partnerships. In a military context, a strategy might be to secure control of a key region. The tactics would then involve the specific movements and deployments of troops and equipment.

Understanding the difference between strategy and tactics is crucial for effective planning and decision-making. Strategy gives you the big-picture plan and direction, while tactics are the actions you take to turn that plan into reality. Both are essential, and their success often depends on how well they align and work together.

We'll dive deeper into tactics in a later chapter, but for now, let's focus on developing a strategic plan. This plan will not only pave the way to achieving your vision but also help you avoid potential pitfalls along the way.

## Why Not to Start with the SWOT Exercise?

The SWOT (Strengths, Weaknesses, Opportunities, and Threats) analysis has been a go-to tool for strategic planning for years. It provides a structured way to assess both the internal and external factors that can impact an organization. But here's the thing—when you're building a true strategic plan, starting with a SWOT analysis might not be the best approach. Instead of diving right into the nitty-gritty of what's working and what's not, it's often more powerful to begin with your vision.

Why? Because SWOT analysis, by its very nature, is introspective. It focuses on the current state of your organization—what's happening right now. While that's important, this focus on the present can sometimes trap you in the status quo. You might find yourself anchored to today's issues and miss the chance to envision bold, transformative strategies that go beyond your current strengths and weaknesses.

I've seen it happen time and again—teams get so caught up in last week's big problems that they miss the larger, more impactful challenges that are holding them back. They end up with a plan that addresses immediate concerns but doesn't move the needle when it comes to long-term growth and innovation.

Starting with the vision shifts the focus. It's about looking forward, not just assessing where you are now but imagining where you want to be. When you begin with a clear vision, you set a destination that guides your entire planning process. From there, you can use tools like SWOT to identify what's helping or hindering your progress towards that vision. But by leading with the vision, you're less likely to get bogged down by current limitations and more likely to think expansively about the future.

So, while SWOT has its place in the planning process, it's not always the best starting point. Begin with your vision—think big, think bold. Once you've got that clear picture of where you want to go, then use SWOT to figure out how to get there. This approach helps ensure that your strategic plan is not just reactive to present issues but proactive and geared towards long-term success.

SWOT can constrain visionary and innovative thinking.

Chris Moore

A SWOT analysis, by its very nature, puts organizations into a predefined box, which can really limit creative and innovative thinking.

It's all about sorting elements into four neat categories—strengths, weaknesses, opportunities, and threats—but this can unintentionally lead to a boxed-in mindset. Instead of encouraging bold, out-of-the-box strategies, it often keeps the focus on what we can do right now, not what we could potentially achieve.

One of the pitfalls of a SWOT analysis is that it tends to overemphasize internal factors—strengths and weaknesses—at the expense of fully exploring and leveraging external factors like opportunities and threats. When you dive straight into a SWOT, you might find yourself getting stuck in the details, dissecting every little strength and weakness, which can lead to what's often called analysis paralysis. You get so caught up in solving today's problems that you lose sight of the bigger picture—the overarching vision you're trying to achieve.

True strategic planning should be about more than just the here and now. It should be visionary. Instead of starting with a SWOT, it's far more effective to begin with a clear and compelling vision, the kind we talked about earlier. This forward-looking focus helps you set ambitious goals that aren't restricted by your current capabilities or challenges.

A vision-centric approach opens the door to innovation and creativity. It allows you to dream big and explore radical ideas that could completely redefine your organization's future, rather than just making incremental improvements on the present. When you start with a clear vision, you align everyone in your organization toward a common goal. This creates a strong sense of purpose and direction, which is essential for effective strategic planning.

With a clear strategy in place, your tactics become much more effective. When everyone in your organization is focused on the same vision, they'll naturally select tactics that move the needle in the right direction. In other words, starting with a vision not only inspires big-picture thinking but also ensures that every step taken along the way is aligned with that ultimate goal. This is how you turn strategy into action and action into success.

"Strategy without tactics is the slowest route to victory. Tactics without strategy is the noise before defeat."

Sun Tzu

While SWOT analysis is definitely valuable, it's best saved for the phase where you're fine-tuning tactics and looking for ways to improve. The real starting point should be your vision and strategy. These should guide the SWOT analysis, ensuring that your focus stays on achieving those long-term goals rather than getting caught up in the current state of affairs.

Strategic planning is absolutely critical for the success and growth of any organization. And while tools like SWOT analysis have their place, they shouldn't take center stage in the early stages of planning. When you start with a clear vision, you're not just reacting to where you are right now—you're aiming for where you want to be in the future. This kind of vision-led approach sparks innovation, aligns everyone in the organization towards a common goal, and helps ensure that the strategies you develop are ambitious and long-term focused.

As you kick off your strategic planning journey, it's important to remember that a powerful vision is the cornerstone of any successful long-term strategy. It's what keeps you looking forward and drives you toward a transformative future, rather than getting stuck in the status quo.

The process starts by clearly defining your vision. What does success look like in the long term? Once that's in place, you can begin mapping out the broad strokes of your strategy. This means identifying the key objectives you need to achieve and the major milestones along the way. From there, you break it down further into specific, actionable steps that will move you closer to your vision.

This is where tools like SWOT analysis come into play—not as the starting point, but as a way to refine your approach. You use SWOT to assess whether your strategy aligns with your strengths, mitigates your weaknesses, takes advantage of opportunities, and prepares you for potential threats. But always keep the bigger picture in mind—the vision is what drives everything.

So, by leading with vision and following up with strategic planning and tactical refinement, you create a roadmap that guides your organization toward that long-term success. It's a journey, but one that's grounded in a clear direction and fueled by a shared commitment to reaching those ambitious goals.

But you might be wondering—how do we actually go from vision to strategy? How do we take that big, inspiring vision and turn it into a concrete plan that gets us to our desired end result, whether that's 5, 10, or 25 years down the road?

## Enter the Pre-Mortem

I want to introduce you to a powerful tool originally designed for project managers working on a single project. It's incredibly handy for project teams, and I highly encourage you to incorporate it into your process. With the right framing, it's straightforward to understand and implement in the vision-to-strategy journey. This tool helps us focus on the future state and the path to get there, ensuring greater success along the way.

If you're around my age, you might remember growing up with the TV show Quincy, M.E., where Quincy, the LA coroner, would look at a body and figure out everything that had happened to that person right before they died, ultimately solving all sorts of crimes. This idea later evolved into the popular CSI-type shows, where crime scene investigators look at the end result and work backward to determine how everything went down. But instead of a post-mortem, we're going to talk about something called a premortem.

The premortem is a brilliant process because, as we've probably heard a million times, hindsight is 20/20. We've all thought, "If only I knew then what I know now, I would've done things differently." The beauty of the premortem is that it allows you to harness that 20/20 hindsight before you even begin. It's like taking a sneak peek into the future to prevent problems before they happen.

So, how does a premortem work in a project setting?

The concept was introduced by Gary Klein, and it represents a major shift in how project teams approach risk management and problem-solving. Unlike the traditional post-mortem, where you look back and analyze what went wrong after a project has failed, the premortem operates on the idea of predictive hindsight. Now, I know it might sound a bit strange—how can you do a post-mortem on a project that hasn't even started? But that's exactly what makes the premortem so valuable.

Here's how it works: a team imagines that the project they're about to begin has already ended in disaster. They then work backward to figure out what could have gone wrong. This proactive approach allows the team to identify potential pitfalls and flawed assumptions before they become real problems.

The strength of the premortem lies in its proactive nature. By assuming failure in a controlled environment, teams can anticipate not just the obvious risks but also the more subtle, often unspoken concerns that could derail the project. It helps to uncover the hidden cracks in the project's foundation—the critical points where things like communication breakdowns, resource shortages, technical issues, and other challenges could emerge and cause major setbacks.

The premortem is rooted in psychological research, particularly in understanding cognitive biases. Traditional risk management techniques often fall victim to groupthink, overconfidence, and other planning failures that can create a false sense of security. The premortem counters these biases by creating a space where skepticism and critical thinking are encouraged. It invites team members to voice doubts and challenge assumptions, which is something that can be tough to do in many team settings.

The best time to conduct a premortem is right at the start of a project, ideally during a kickoff meeting when the plan is still flexible, and everyone's energy is high. It injects a healthy dose of realism into the excitement that comes with launching a new project. By balancing enthusiasm with a careful consideration of what could go wrong, the team can create a more resilient and robust plan.

## Using the Pre-Mortem for Long-Term Strategy

It's time to revisit your vision, but don't do it alone. Gather your most trusted allies—this isn't just about your executive or management team. Bring in your family, your closest advisors, and a mix of people who bring different perspectives to the table.

You want a diverse group: free-thinkers, dreamers, strategic minds, marketers, risk managers, risk-takers, operations folks, and people who know your industry inside and out, as well as those with experience in other fields. The key here is to create an environment where everyone feels free to explore and discuss. No idea is too small, and nothing is too grand.

Here's what you'll need: a big stack of Post-it notes and plenty of wall space.

Before the meeting, make sure everyone has a printed copy of your vision and understands the premortem process. Encourage them to spend a few days thinking about it and jotting down some notes.

When you get together, start by reading your vision aloud to the group. Let people stop you if they have questions or need something clarified.

Now, here's the fun part: Imagine it's 20-25 years in the future (or 10 years, if that's your exit plan). You've reached your vision, and everything has gone perfectly. Your team should start writing down what happened along the way on those Post-it notes. These should be the Big Rocks—the major milestones and achievements that paved the road to success.

Don't worry about creating a detailed, step-by-step project plan, and don't worry about putting things in order just yet. Encourage your strategy team to think big and to think about the journey from start to finish. This exercise is about capturing the essence of the path you'll take, setting the stage for more detailed planning down the line.

The goal is to tell the story of how you got from where you are now to where you want to be. How did everything build up to this moment of success?

Here are some examples from other people I have worked with:

- *We moved operations from California to Texas to be closer to our market. Our people were there.*

- *I was mentored by a Fortune 500 CEO founder who took his company national. He gave me the knowledge, contacts, and courage to do it too.*

- *A celebrity started using our product. Joined the board and became our spokesperson.*

- *Our product went viral on social media and gave us brand recognition.*

- *We bought a larger but stagnant business with the manufacturing capability, but they needed to learn how to sell. We always knew how to sell it, but they gave us the margins we needed and control of the inventory.*

- *We expanded our income by licensing our tech and patents in the European market. It cost us very little and gave us the cash flow needed to grow in the US and Canada.*

- *We were listed in Forbes's Top 100 Places to Work and had the best talent coming to us.*

Have everyone take turns reading their Post-it notes aloud, then work together to arrange them on the wall in the order of events. The timeline that forms will be a mix of everyone's ideas, creating an extensive, intertwined narrative. It doesn't have to be perfect—just place things where they generally seem to fit.

Once that's done, revisit each section of your vision—covering the business, the customers, the team, the industry, and the community. Ask yourselves: Is there anything missing that should be added to the timeline? Are there any gaps that need filling in?

After that, take a moment to celebrate what you've accomplished so far. This is a big step, so give yourselves a well-deserved break. Don't forget to snap some photos of the timeline on the wall; those Post-its have a habit of falling off when you least expect it!

Now, it's time to regroup and dive back in, but this time, focus on what could go wrong. Imagine you're in that same future, but instead of success, everything has gone off the rails. What happened? This is where your risk management thinkers will really shine—it's why you need them in the room. Your action-takers might express regrets about the things you knew you should have done but didn't, maybe because you were too cautious or scared.

This exercise is all about exploring potential pitfalls so that you can better prepare for them. It's not just about imagining failure; it's about learning from it before it happens.

Here are some other examples of failure:

- *We were sued for a product liability claim and didn't have the money or the documentation to fight it.*

- *We never could find good people who would stay. Our stores were never fully staffed.*

- *Our marketing plan was a bust. We spent bad money after worse.*

- *We didn't keep up with technology changes, and our product was obsolete right as we expanded distribution.*

- *We used too much debt to expand, Payments were so high that one bad year shut us down.*

- *I never listened to my advisors or managers. I hired people I didn't trust or believe in, which cost me a lot.*

Alright, this next part might be a bit tough. As we talk through what could go wrong, some of the challenges your business is currently facing might come up. But here's the key—this isn't the time to dive into those issues. Stay focused on the future, as if you're looking back from that point.

We'll take these potential pitfalls and post them on a separate wall labeled "Failure Points."

Here's the question we need to ask: How can we prevent these things from happening? How can we reduce the risks or eliminate them altogether? These are the roadblocks that could get in the way of our growth—the danger signs we need to watch out for.

Let's write down the solutions on Post-it notes and add them to our Success Timeline. We're looking to build a clear path that takes these risks into account and works around them.

Is there anything in the vision that still needs a failure point identified? If so, now's the time to address it.

Let's take one last look at the Success Timeline. Is there anything you want to add based on the failure points we discussed? Did anything new come to mind that should be included?

This is the moment to speak up if you have something to add. Let's make sure we've covered all our bases before we wrap up.

> The pre-mortem exercise gives us a list of things to do and things to not do. Using the power of hindsight, we see the path and the potholes that lead to achieving our vision.
>
> Chris Moore

Is there anything on the wall that we need to rearrange? If everything looks good, let's move on to identifying the Big Rocks and categorizing them.

Grab a marker that stands out against the Post-its, and let's start defining the Big Rocks. These are the things that absolutely have to happen for you to reach your vision.

For example, does that celebrity endorsement need to happen? If you're a women's makeup brand, maybe it does. If not, perhaps your Big Rock is having a strong advertising presence. You might need a powerful campaign that can take you from being a local brand to a regional, and eventually, a national player. Remember, we're talking about Big Rock strategies here—keep it big. You don't need to get into the details or name names just yet.

Now that we've identified the Big Rocks, let's take it a step further. For each Big Rock, think about 1-3 smaller steps you should take to accomplish that goal.

For instance, let's say your Big Rock is launching a strong campaign to transition from a local to a national brand. One step could be finding a company that can represent you on a national level. You might start by researching your options—maybe there's a regional powerhouse that's growing and has one national client under its belt. If they're a good cultural fit and understand your market, this could be your best choice. On the other hand, a small digital marketing firm that just opened last year might not be able to get you where you need to go if your goal is to become a national brand.

The idea here is to break down each Big Rock into actionable steps that move you closer to your ultimate goal. Keep the focus on what will make the biggest impact and drive your success forward.

Here is the last step in our exercise.

## What Big Rocks should we focus on, and what must we accomplish in the next three years?

As a small business owner, if there's a specific company, CEO, or individual you envision being crucial to your future success, then part of your strategy has to be about connecting with them or becoming part of their network. How do you do that? You might need to move to a different neighborhood, join the same gym, or switch to the same CPA or financial advisor. Find out what conferences they attend or events they're likely to be at. This needs to be part of your strategy and tactics for the coming year.

For instance, if your goal is to build relationships with other CEOs who could help distribute your product, plan to attend at least three key events this year where those CEOs will be present. It's as straightforward as that. That's one of your objectives for the year, a step that will pave the way for long-term success.

As you map out these goals, also consider the things you'd rather avoid but know you need to do. It's about following your strategic path and staying committed to what will move you forward.

You probably have a go-to book, like 4DX, Traction, or another favorite on strategic implementation. But maybe you've felt something was missing—like it wasn't getting you where you wanted to go fast enough. The issue often lies in the inputs at the beginning of the process. Whatever works for you and fits your business culture is fine, and I'm not advocating for one method over another. What's crucial is having a defined process that you'll actually follow and use as part of your business operating system.

What can hold back an operating system is misalignment between Vision and Strategy, or a Culture and Team that doesn't support them.

In the next few chapters, we'll dive into culture, team development, and some practical tactics to help you execute the strategy you've developed. Let's make sure everything is aligned so you can achieve your vision faster and more effectively.

# Chapter 9

---

# A Culture that Wins

"Culture eats strategy for breakfast."

Peter Drucker

Y OU'VE GOT YOUR VISION, your strategy, and a clear understanding of the customers you want to reach. Now, it's time to focus on something just as crucial: building a culture that aligns with your goals. This culture should serve your customers in the way they want and need, while also attracting, motivating, and retaining the team that will help bring your vision to life.

As the leader of your organization, you hold the power and responsibility to shape the world you work in. Your culture should be a reflection of your vision. The team you hire and the customers you serve should not only support your goals but also bring you satisfaction and fulfillment. In the long run—through both good times and tough ones—the culture you create will be what drives your vision forward. If you want to "Get Things Done," then build a culture that's capable of doing just that, even without you being there every day.

Every single day, you should take action that reinforces the culture you're trying to build. If you find yourself disliking the people you work with, the customers you serve, or the environment you've created, there's no one else to blame but yourself. Often, we're our own biggest obstacle when it comes to establishing the culture we desire.

If you dread going to work, it's time to take a step back and reflect. Take a day off and look in the mirror. The culture you're struggling with is a result of your leadership. But here's the good news: you also have the power to change it. You are the catalyst for creating a workplace you're proud to own and where your ideal team members want to work and thrive.

So, ask yourself: what kind of environment do you want to build? What kind of culture will not only execute your vision but also make you excited to come to work every day? It's up to you to create that place—where you and your team can succeed together.

---

### Culture = Execution

---

Execution has been a hot topic for decades. Entire books are dedicated to processes, goal setting, data analytics, and a hundred other tactics to ensure things get done. Most all neglect the primary driver of execution – Culture.

"If you have the right people, doing the right things for the right reasons, headed in the right direction, they will make the right decisions at the right time in order to execute what you need done to accomplish your strategy. This is what allows you to achieve your vision." – Chris Moore

Business culture is the heartbeat of your organization—it's the values, behaviors, customs, and beliefs that shape how your company operates day in and day out. It's not just about what you do, but how you do it. Culture encompasses your company's mission, values, and goals, as well as the habits and behaviors of everyone who works there. It's influenced by a mix of things: your company's history, the industry you're in, the values of your founders and leadership team, and even the broader cultural norms of the country and region where your company is based.

Why is culture so important? Because it directly impacts employee satisfaction, motivation, and ultimately, the success of your business.

A positive culture can fuel teamwork, creativity, and innovation, while a negative one can drag down morale, increase turnover, and hurt performance. As a business leader, you have a huge role in shaping and maintaining this culture by setting the tone, establishing expectations, and modeling the behaviors you want to see.

Different businesses define their culture in various ways. Here are some examples:

- *"We're a family business, and we want it to feel like a family picnic every day."*

- *"We're a professional organization, and we'll always act like it."*

- *"No drama. Just get your work done. If someone's a drama queen or can't get their stuff done, I cut them loose quickly."*

- *"I guess we're old school, but we stick to pen and paper."*

- *"We're always on the cutting edge. We love new tech and new toys."*

What's common across all these businesses? The understanding that if a potential team member doesn't fit the culture, their skills alone won't be enough. The culture is the filter through which everything and everyone passes. It's what distinguishes one company from another.

Technology can give you an edge, but it's not enough on its own. Marketing can get you noticed, but it can only take you so far. What really sets your company apart is your culture. It's the glue that holds everything together and the engine that drives your business forward. When your culture is strong and aligned with your vision, it becomes a powerful force that can propel your business to new heights.

**Brands can fail and disappear overnight.**

Nokia made an outstanding, virtually indestructible product, yet they disappeared from the market. Motorola and Blackberry, despite having amazing products and a large customer base, didn't win the phone wars either. So, what went wrong?

In the end, it all comes down to culture. The one thing that truly sets a company apart is its culture. Products, strategies, and pricing can all be copied by competitors. What can't be replicated are the beliefs, attitudes, and everyday focus of your workforce that make your company unique. It's your company's individuality that stands out and gives you an edge.

Culture can mean different things depending on who you ask. It might be your brand, your motto, your values, the way people dress, or the habits that form within your team. But at its core, culture is about attitudes, beliefs, actions, and norms. It's not just about what you say—it's about what you do and the environment you create.

Every organization has a culture, whether it's a small business or a giant corporation. In an unhealthy culture, employees operate as individuals, just trying to get through the day or doing the bare minimum to meet their own needs. This kind of organization is usually reactive, with a culture that formed by accident rather than by design. In these cases, culture isn't managed—it just happens.

On the other hand, a healthy corporate culture recognizes every individual, regardless of their role, and encourages them to work together as a team. In a positive culture, everyone is united in a work environment that benefits both the company and its employees. A strong culture fosters values that boost performance by motivating people and guiding their actions toward a shared goal.

Your company's culture starts with you and is carried forward by your employees. It's a reflection of who you are. How you treat your staff will shape how they treat each other and your customers. This process begins the moment they walk through your door and continues to grow and evolve over time.

So, what do you do to teach someone about your company and the message you want to convey to your customers? How do you train employees on your expectations, and how do you reinforce or correct their performance? All of these elements are part of your culture.

Ultimately, it's your culture that determines whether your company thrives or struggles, and it is a process that requires ongoing attention and effort.

## Practical Steps to Build Culture

Here are some practical steps you can take to shape and strengthen your business culture:

1. **Define Your Values and Mission:** Start with a clear foundation—your values and mission. These are the cornerstones of your business culture. Clearly express what your organization stands for and what it aims to achieve. Your culture and mission should go hand in hand. When your team is passionate about your mission and values, they'll be driven to achieve the goals that support your purpose. But if people are just clocking in for a paycheck or to get through the day, you'll never instill the passion needed to reach your full potential.

2. **Communicate Your Values and Mission:** Make sure everyone on your team understands your values and mission and sees how they fit into the bigger picture. This helps

create a sense of purpose and belonging. Develop a process to introduce new hires to your culture and explain how you envision the company working together.

3. **Hire for Cultural Fit:** When bringing new people on board, look for those who align with your values and who will thrive in your culture. It's about more than just skills—it's about finding people who are compatible with your work environment and who will contribute positively to the team.

4. **Encourage Teamwork and Collaboration:** Create an environment where teamwork and collaboration are the norms. Ask yourself: what does your ideal workplace look like? Make it supportive, inclusive, and a place where people enjoy working together.

5. **Provide Opportunities for Growth:** Invest in your team by offering opportunities for learning and development. Whether it's through training programs, workshops, or professional development, helping your employees grow will benefit both them and your business.

6. **Reinforce Your Culture:** Think about the little things that can reinforce your culture daily. Maybe it's posters that reflect your values, company gatherings, or something as

simple as pizza on Fridays. I've seen companies where morning shout-outs or group activities set the tone for the day. Whether it's a high five, a "Go Team!" cheer, or a reward like a candy bar for a job well done, these small gestures go a long way in building a strong culture.

7. **Recognize and Reward Good Performance:** Show appreciation for employees who contribute positively to your organization and its culture. Recognition programs, promotions, and bonuses are all great ways to do this. It's about making sure people feel valued for their hard work and dedication.

8. **Encourage Open Communication:** Create a culture where open and honest communication is valued. Encourage everyone to contribute ideas and feedback. While you, as the owner, guide the company, it's essential to listen to your team. Ask them what they like about the culture, what they don't, and what ideas they have for improvement. You hired them for their skills and expertise—make sure you're tapping into what they have to offer.

9. **Model the Behavior You Want to See:** As a leader, your actions set the tone. Be intentional about how you interact with your staff because your attitude and behavior will influ-

ence them. Remember, your culture is shaped by what you do, not just what you say. You may know exactly what you want to achieve and how to get there, but it's crucial to be deliberate in delivering that message. Don't let frustration or fatigue drive your actions—lead with purpose and consistency.

By following these steps, you'll be well on your way to developing a strong, positive business culture that not only supports your success but also makes your company a place where people want to work and grow.

> ### *Remember, culture cannot be imitated. It can only be made.*

Just like understanding your customers is crucial for success, so is cultivating a vibrant and engaging company culture. Your culture is the soul of your business, shaping employee experience, attracting talent, and ultimately impacting your bottom line. But defining your desired culture goes beyond ping pong tables and casual Fridays. It delves deeper, encompassing values, behaviors, and aspirations that create a unique and thriving work environment.

Just like your vision, you need to have a clear and complete description of your company culture. Here is a quick guide to help get you started.

# Company Culture Development Guide

## Core Values

What are the fundamental principles that guide your decision-making and actions? (e.g., Innovation, Integrity, Collaboration, Sustainability)

How do these values translate into tangible behaviors within your company?

How do you attract and retain employees who embody these values?

## Mission and Vision

What is your company's purpose beyond just making money? What impact do you strive to create on the world?

What does your vision statement say about your desired future state? How does it translate into cultural aspirations?

How do your mission and vision inspire and motivate your employees?

## Work Environment

What kind of atmosphere do you want to create? Collaborative, fast-paced, creative, fun, results-oriented?

What physical space and amenities contribute to your desired environment? (e.g., open office, flexible work arrangements, wellness facilities)

How do you foster open communication and transparency within your team?

## Work-Life Balance and Employee Recognition

What does work-life balance look like in your company? Do you offer flexible hours, remote work options, or generous vacation policies?

How do you recognize and reward employee achievements? Public recognition, bonuses, career development opportunities?

How do you ensure employees feel valued and appreciated? Regular feedback, growth opportunities, positive reinforcement?

## Leadership and Management

What qualities and behaviors define your ideal leaders and managers? (e.g., Empathy, communication, delegation, empowerment)

How do leaders and managers promote and embody your desired culture?

What training and development opportunities do you offer to equip leaders with the necessary skills?

## Feedback and Communication

How do you encourage open and honest feedback within your team? (e.g., regular surveys, anonymous feedback channels, one-on-one meetings)

How do you ensure information flows freely across all levels of the organization?

How do you create a culture where constructive criticism is accepted and valued?

## Learning and Growth

Do you offer opportunities for professional development and skill-building? (e.g., training programs, conferences, mentorship programs)

How do you encourage employees to take ownership of their learning and growth?

How do you foster a culture of continuous improvement and innovation?

## Celebration and Fun

How do you celebrate team successes and milestones? (e.g., team outings, company events, recognition programs)

How do you incorporate fun and humor into your work environment? (e.g., team-building activities, social events, casual dress code)

How do you ensure everyone feels included and valued during celebrations?

## Social Responsibility and Community

What are your company's values regarding social responsibility and community engagement? (e.g., Volunteering, environmental sustainability, philanthropic initiatives)

How do you involve employees in your social responsibility efforts?

How does your community engagement align with your overall culture and values?

Remember, your company culture is a living, breathing entity that evolves over time. Regularly revisit and refine your definition to ensure it remains relevant and reflects the aspirations of your team. By carefully defining and nurturing your desired culture, you can create a work environment that attracts and retains top talent, fuels innovation, and propels your business toward achieving your vision.

# Chapter 10

---

# Team – The Scarcest Resource

"The single most powerful asset any company has is its workforce. People are not your most important asset. The right people are."

Jim Collins

Y OU HAVE PROBABLY BEEN to multiple locations of the same franchise and noticed a difference. They have the same products, services, processes, software, training materials, and marketing and advertising plans. That is, after all, why you buy a franchise. You get all the ingredients for a proven, successful business.

So why are they not all successful?

Team and the culture of that team. Admittedly, leadership is where the responsibility hangs, but this is your missing ingredient as a leader. The team you hire and the culture you create differentiate one location from another. In many franchise systems, why does one location never cross $1 million in sales while another does 5x or even 20x that amount? The leader never develops the team and culture to support that level of business, or that can serve the customers how they need to be served to succeed.

Let's face it, finding the right people to join your team is tough. It's not just about their skills or how many years they've been in the game. It's more about finding people who understand your company and are excited to help push the mission forward. These are the people who not only do great work but also bring out the best in everyone around them.

It's like putting together a great band where every member plays their part perfectly but also vibes with the group. You will see how creating a positive, inclusive team environment isn't just good for morale. It's your secret weapon in attracting customers and more team members who love what you're all about.

Because, in the end, it's the people who make all the difference. Let's figure out how to find them, keep them, and grow together.

When hiring and developing your team, it can become easy to over-look cultural fit. We tend to value experience and knowledge and ignore everything else if we think an individual can solve a current problem or fill an open role. This may solve one issue but cause many more.

I want to use a fictitious example that we all can relate to. Remember Major Charles Emerson Winchester III from MASH? He famously said, "I do one thing. I do it well. Then I move on." This mindset worked brilliantly for him at a prestigious Boston hospital, where excellence in a narrow specialty was valued above all. But when he joined the MASH unit, his approach didn't fit the team or the situation.

> "I do one thing. I do it well. Then I move on."
> Major Charles Emerson Winchester III (Character in
> MASH)

Charles valued excellence and perfection above all else. What the team needed was speed. Without speed and the right priorities, people died. Charles had never been in this world. This is a prime example of how someone can be top-notch in their field but still not be the right fit for a team's culture. The MAS*H unit thrived on versatility, collaboration, and the ability to adapt quickly to changing circumstances—a stark contrast to the rigid, specialized excellence of Winchester's Boston backdrop. For Winchester, the transition was tough. He was used to being a lone star. Still, the unit needed him to be a team player, adapt, and broaden his horizons beyond his single-minded focus on surgical excellence.

What if leadership had guided him prior to placing him in that situation, the culture, and how it would require him to adapt? How would that have affected both him and the overall enterprise?

Winchester's struggle and eventual adaptation highlight a crucial business lesson: fitting into the company culture is just as important as professional expertise. It's about finding people with the skills and the adaptability to mesh well with the team's way of working and values. Like Winchester had to learn to adjust his approach to succeed in the MAS*H unit, companies must seek out individuals who can thrive in their cultural environment.

This story serves as a reminder that building a successful team is not just about collecting individuals with impressive resumes. It's about creating a harmonious group that works well together, supports each other, and shares a common vision. So, as we think about assembling our dream teams, let's remember to consider what each person can do and how they'll fit into the broader tapestry of our company culture. Because in the end, the strength of a team lies not just in the talents of its members but in their ability to come together and create something greater than the sum of their parts.

Our business is built by our teams. If the company is built by you, it's totally dependent upon you. Initially, we need to know how everything works, but ultimately, you need to not be the smartest person in the room. You also don't need to do everything. There's no way to scale because it is only you and the limited time you have to give. You're trading time for money; ultimately, you're just trading time and not even making money. We can't sustain that way.

"Talent wins games, but teamwork and intelligence win championships."

Michael Jordan

Our team is everything, and how we develop that team is just as crucial. To build a truly effective team, we need to understand the dynamics at play. It's about recognizing what makes a high-performing team tick and fostering a culture that supports it. Every part of your business plays a role in turning your vision into reality, and your team is right at the heart of that.

Let's go back to your compelling vision for the future. Picture yourself in that future state. You started by envisioning what your business would look like and who your customers would be. But an essential part of that vision is your team—the people who will help you get there.

Your team has to be aligned with that long-term vision, whether it's 10, 15, or even 25 years down the road. Yes, you need customers who will buy your products and services and provide the revenue to achieve your goals. But just as importantly, you need a team that can support and grow with those customers. Your vision isn't just about what you're building—it's about who's building it with you. The right team will be the driving force behind your success, working together to turn that vision into a reality.

**So what does the team and the culture look like?**

Let's say I have a highly intelligent customer who expects nothing less than highly intelligent service. To meet that expectation, I'm going to need a team that's equally smart and capable of delivering that level of service. Maybe the customer is looking for an upscale, white-glove experience. We have to make sure our team is equipped to support those needs and deliver on the promises we make in our vision.

Now, before anyone gets the wrong idea, I'm not talking about race, religion, disabilities, or any other protected characteristics. This is all about knowing your customers and being able to serve them effectively.

A few years ago, I spoke with a business owner who bought an existing company in the heart of Koreatown in Los Angeles—a diverse area with a strong Korean and Latino presence. He knew that the business needed more face-to-face marketing, so he hired an experienced "rainmaker" with a stellar track record from multiple other locations. But despite the salesperson's experience, he failed to connect in Koreatown.

Why? It all came down to culture and language. Most of the business owners in the area were Korean and Latino. While many spoke some English, they were much more comfortable doing business in their native languages.

So, what did the owner do? He didn't just throw up his hands. Instead, he adapted. The "hired gun" salesperson returned to his previous employer, and the owner hired a friend of one of his technicians—a guy who spoke English, Korean, and Spanish but had no formal sales experience beyond answering phones. The owner was impressed from the start; the new hire was outgoing, personable, and detail-oriented.

The owner went out with his new salesperson to meet current customers, introducing him and asking for feedback on how they could improve the customer experience. They quickly realized they needed to translate their sales materials and service contracts into Korean and Spanish. They signed the new salesperson up for sales training and even arranged for him to do ride-alongs with the previous "expert" to gain some on-the-job experience.

It didn't take long before they started seeing real growth and building the new relationships they needed. The owner also made sure to have service technicians who spoke English, Korean, and Spanish available on every shift, so customers always had someone they could communicate with comfortably.

The result? The business tripled its revenue in just 18 months.

The lesson here is clear: understanding your customers and having the right team in place to serve them is key to success. It's about more than just filling a role—it's about finding people who can connect with your customers and deliver the experience you've promised.

**Let's start by asking ourselves, who do I need? Who do I need to support this customer?**

I've had the privilege of visiting companies all over the country, many of them franchises in the exact same business, offering the exact same products and services. Yet, what stands out is how different their cultures and team members can be. The common thread? The owners set the tone.

I've walked into some of these businesses where everything is highly professional, with a calm, reserved, white-glove experience. It's like stepping into a British upper-crust environment, where everything is polished and proper, and that's how they operate—it's their culture. Then, I've been to other franchises in the same industry that are just as successful but operate completely differently. In these places, it's all about energy—team members are chest-thumping, high-fiving, shouting nicknames, and making it feel like a party all day long.

Both of these businesses are successful, but they're serving slightly different customer bases, and they've built their teams to support their unique cultures and deliver their services at a high level. It's the culture, the personality, and the specific skill set of the team that make it work.

So, who do you need on your team? Think about the kind of people who will thrive in your environment and help you reach your vision. Start by mapping out your organizational chart—what roles do you need to fill to get where you want to go? And then, take a look at who you already have on your team.

Take stock of your current team. What are their strengths? Are there any gaps? And if there are, ask yourself if it's a gap you need to fill by hiring someone new, or is it something that could be addressed with the right training? Sometimes, it's just a matter of giving people the right opportunities to grow and succeed.

Remember, your culture needs to serve three key areas: your business, your customers, and your team. It's about finding the right balance that serves your vision and keeps your customers satisfied.

What do your customers need? What kind of experience should they have? And what kind of team do you need to deliver that experience?

When you're hiring and building out your team, it's important to have a strategy in place to attract, interview, and retain the best talent—the team members who will help you achieve your goals and fulfill your strategic plan. Think about this from a strategic standpoint. It's not just about the specific ads you place; it's about clearly communicating your culture and what you're looking for.

If you're working with an HR person or a hiring agency, you need to be able to tell them, "Here's what our culture is like. Here's what our customer looks like. Here's what our business is about, and this is what you can expect when you work here." By being clear about your culture and needs, you'll attract the right people who will help you build the business you envision.

## Team Roles, Responsibilities and Culture

How do your team's roles and responsibilities align with the big vision and their part in achieving it? This is especially crucial for your executive and management teams. Do they understand how they add value to the organization? When you're evaluating their performance, are you considering how well they're moving toward that shared vision and how effectively they're fulfilling their role within it?

Take a look at your written Roles and Responsibilities—do they include your vision and culture? In my experience, most training on roles and responsibilities focuses on checklists of tasks and accountability metrics. Sure, they usually touch on providing excellent customer service, being responsive, and other buzzwords, but often, there's no real depth or explanation. Just like when you communicate your vision, your roles and responsibilities need to be more meaningful.

So, here's what I suggest: Create a question-and-answer document that you'll use throughout the hiring, development, and evaluation phases of team building. For every position, you or your management team should fill this out. This document will also guide you when creating onboarding and training for each role. Make sure every topic is covered and provides clear answers for the new hire. They should receive a blank copy and understand that these are the things they need to learn in the next 30, 60, or 90 days—whatever timeframe you set. Their manager or trainer should also be familiar with these answers and be responsible for teaching them, whether it's operating a machine or running a register. Every role needs this clarity. You might need to add specific details based on your business, but the core idea remains the same.

Now, take a moment to answer these questions for your current role. Something tells me it might be challenging, or you'll have to think hard to give a solid answer. So, how much more important is it that your team understands these concepts?

Imagine how things would change if each team member had a clear understanding of these questions. How would that clarity transform your business?

# How Your Role Connects: A Personal Roadmap to Alignment

Understanding your role's impact within the company is crucial for both your personal satisfaction and organizational success. This outline will guide you in exploring how your specific position:

- **Fits into and provides value to the company vision:**

  - *Company Vision Breakdown:*

    - Clearly state the company's vision statement and core values.

    - °Briefly explain the overall strategic goals.

  - *Your Role's Contribution:*

    - Identify key responsibilities and objectives of your position.

    - Explain how your daily tasks directly contribute to achieving the broader company goals.

    - Highlight specific metrics or outcomes your work helps achieve.

    - Quantify the value you create, e.g., increased revenue,

improved customer satisfaction, etc.

- *Impact on the Bigger Picture:*

  - Connect your individual contributions to the company's overall impact.

  - Explain how your role helps fulfill the company's purpose and make a positive difference.

- **Integrates into the customer journey:**

  - *Customer Persona Deep Dive:*

    - Describe the primary customer personas your company serves.

    - Understand their needs, challenges, and desires.

  - *Your Role's Touchpoints:*

    - Identify all points in the customer journey where your role interacts with customers, directly or indirectly.

    - Explain how your actions affect the customer experience.

    - Highlight opportunities to add value and improve their satisfaction.

○ *Contribution to Success:*

- Demonstrate how your role contributes to a smooth and positive customer journey.

- Explain how your efforts ultimately lead to customer acquisition, retention, and loyalty.

- **Aligns with your aspirations and company needs:**

○ *Your Personal Vision:*

- Define your career goals and aspirations.

- Identify the skills and experiences you want to develop.

○ *Company Growth Trajectory:*

- Understand the company's plans for growth and expansion.

- Identify emerging needs and challenges.

○ *Alignment Opportunities:*

- Show how your aspirations and skills align with the company's needs and growth trajectory.

- Highlight areas where you can contribute to future goals and overcome challenges.

- Address any areas where your aspirations might require further development or adjustment.

○ *Mutual Growth:*

- Explain how working towards the company vision helps you achieve your personal goals.

- Emphasize the opportunities for learning and development provided by the company.

- Show how your continued growth benefits both yourself and the organization.

By completing this outline, you will understand the significance of your role, its impact on customers, and its alignment with your personal aspirations. This will empower you to work with greater purpose, motivation, and a clear sense of how your individual contributions contribute to the company's success.

## One Last Note about Your Culture

You've probably heard the saying, "People leave managers, not companies." There's a lot of truth to that. A manager sets the course for their team, making sure everyone's rowing in the same direction and helping them navigate the chaos of the day. But if a manager is pushing a different culture, set of roles, or business vision than what you've established, they're actually working against the culture you've worked so hard to create—and the great people you've put under their care. When that happens, problems crop up fast, and your best team members might start looking for the door.

Managers have a huge impact on whether the work atmosphere feels right. They set the tone and the vibe of the workplace and can turn a good team into a great one. Their job isn't to create their own vibe but to amplify the culture that's already in place, guiding everyone toward the shared goal.

It's not just about getting the job done—it's about how everyone feels while doing it. A good manager ensures that the team not only meets its goals but also enjoys the journey. Even the toughest jobs can feel rewarding when the culture supports the team. Managers who get this right reinforce what the company stands for, making everyone feel like they're part of something bigger. When this happens, people don't just stick around—they help build a thriving, attractive culture that makes your company a great place to work and a place customers are drawn to.

As your company grows, adding effective managers to your team becomes crucial. You might already have several layers of management, and they play a key role in establishing and maintaining your corporate culture. So, how do you ensure your managers embody the right traits and pass them on to their teams?

I recommend John Maxwell's book Developing the Leaders Around You. The best way to lead and influence others is to focus on improving yourself while also helping others grow. On page 99, Maxwell outlines his Five-Step Process of Training People, which I'll summarize below:

I Model – I show them how I want it done.

I Mentor – I work with them to help them understand the how and why.

I Monitor – I help them do it on their own and have them explain it back to me.

I Motivate – I encourage them and help them improve.

I Multiply – I get them to teach the skill to someone else.

After going through this process, Maxwell suggests giving your managers the "Big Three": Responsibility, Authority, and Accountability.

Many of us are quick to hold people accountable, but taking the time to guide them through these five steps is far more challenging—and far more rewarding. If you focus on these steps and make sure you've fully completed them before handing over responsibility and accountability, your management and leadership skills will improve, and your company's culture will transform. It takes daily, intentional action to achieve this, but it's worth it for you and your business.

As your company grows, having excellent managers will be one of the most critical factors in your employees' success. After all, employees leave managers, not companies. You want managers who are experienced, mature, dynamic, and capable of leading the way. Establish clear expectations and conduct regular reviews.

The difference between a good company and a great one often comes down to the people who work there and the culture they cultivate. Even the most skilled individuals need to align with the team's culture to excel and contribute to the organization's success.

As leaders, it's our job to create an environment where everyone can thrive, bringing their unique strengths to the table while working in harmony toward a shared vision. A team that's aligned in purpose and action is unstoppable. Finding and nurturing the right team might seem daunting, but the rewards of getting it right are immeasurable.

Ultimately, our success isn't just measured by the milestones we achieve—it's about the lives we touch along the way. It's about turning challenges into opportunities for growth, celebrating shared victories, and building a culture of unity and purpose. Let's build our businesses and lives with a clear vision, a commitment to our team, and a resolve to create a culture that makes us proud to come to work every day.

# Chapter 11

---

# Tactics for Execution

"Success doesn't necessarily come from breakthrough innovation but from flawless execution."

Naveen Jain

N ow, WE'VE FINALLY ARRIVED at the stage where most people start: execution.

So, why do most businesses begin here? It's simple: execution is where the rubber meets the road. It's the part that gives the customer what they want, which, in theory, should lead to more sales. Business owners love checklists and done-for-you services because they offer a sense of accomplishment. But after 3-6 months, many give up because the execution tactic didn't deliver the results they were hoping for.

Here are the **top 10 reasons why businesses often struggle to execute** on their goals:

1. **Lack of Clear Vision and Strategy:** Without a clear direction, it's hard for a business to execute effectively. Employees need to understand where the company is headed and how their work contributes to getting there.

2. **Poor Communication:** When communication is lacking, misunderstandings and misaligned priorities can throw off execution. This includes communication from top management to employees and between different departments.

3. **Resistance to Change:** Internal resistance can crop up when trying to implement new strategies. This resistance might come from fear of the unknown, a loss of control, or just a preference for the status quo.

4. **Inadequate Resources:** Limited resources—whether financial, human, or technological—can severely hinder a company's ability to execute. This could mean not having enough skilled people, funding for projects, or up-to-date technology.

5. **Poor Leadership and Management:** Leadership is crucial for successful execution. Weak leadership can result in a lack of direction, low morale, and poor decision-making. Similarly, ineffective management practices can stifle productivity and innovation.

6. **Lack of Accountability:** When there's no accountability, it breeds complacency. Without a sense of responsibility, execution efforts can easily fall apart.

7. **Ineffective Planning and Project Management:** Poorly defined goals, unrealistic timelines, and inadequate risk management can derail execution. Good planning and project management are essential for staying on track and meeting objectives.

8. **Failure to Adapt to Market Changes:** Businesses that don't keep an eye on the external environment and adapt to market shifts, consumer preferences, or technology changes risk falling behind their competitors.

9. **Overloaded Agendas:** Trying to do too much at once can spread resources too thin and lead to burnout. Prioritizing objectives and focusing on a manageable number of initiatives is key to improving execution.

10. **Cultural Misalignment:** If the company culture doesn't align with the strategy or doesn't support the behaviors needed for execution, it can become a major obstacle. Culture shapes how employees work and interact, and it can either help or hinder execution.

If you look closely, you'll notice that many of these issues are addressed when you focus on Vision and Culture and make them a priority in your business. A well-defined vision guides you to the right strategy, and a deliberately crafted culture that supports both the vision and strategy makes execution much smoother. By following the steps we've outlined in this book, you and your team will have a clear understanding of where you're headed and how you plan to get there. You'll be part of one cohesive team with a shared culture, holding each other accountable to the group's values and goals.

There are three remaining challenges we need to tackle, and even these are interconnected: ineffective planning and project management, overloaded agendas, and inadequate resources. To address these, we need a process that ensures we're focusing on the right things in the right order and not overwhelming our team.

By getting these elements right—vision, culture, planning, and resource management—you'll set the stage for successful execution, ensuring your business not only survives but thrives.

I like to use Peter Drucker's Management by Objective (MBO) process for this task. In a nutshell, management sets the objective, and then the team responsible for executing it figures out what needs to be done and how best to measure success. You could think of it this way: management sets the "lag" KPI goal, and the team helps define the "lead" measures and the action plan to achieve it. Don't worry if you're not familiar with lag and lead measures—we'll dive into those, along with data analytics and key performance metrics, in a future chapter.

As a practical guide, you'll set the goal and choose the team members who will work to achieve it.

The Management by Objective process is all about making sure we're focusing on the right things. For bigger projects—like developing a new process, training, launching new technology or products, or opening a new location—you might need to break it down into implementation sprints, or even a series of them. We'll get into that in the next chapter.

## What Is Management by Objective?

Management by Objective is a structured approach that allows management to zero in on achievable goals and get the best possible results from the resources available. It's designed to help managers avoid getting trapped in day-to-day activities—what we often call the "whirlwind"—where it's easy to lose sight of the primary purpose and objectives.

Peter Drucker first introduced the concept of Management by Objective in his 1954 book The Practice of Management. He described it as a process for setting challenging but attainable objectives and motivating employees to work toward the company's goals. However, Drucker also pointed out that MBO isn't a magic fix for all management problems. It only works if everyone knows what the objective is. The reality is, 90% of the time, the people doing the actual work don't even know the objective they're supposed to be reaching. So, no matter how well you set your goals or how often you follow up, if your team isn't clear on what they're working towards, your chances of success are slim.

## What Are Objectives?

Objectives are statements of desired outcomes or expectations. Think of it like this: You start with a big goal, a lofty idea—something significant you want to achieve. Maybe you want to open a new location, perhaps in another city, or start offering a new service line. To reach that big goal, you need to set smaller objectives, which are the stepping stones that will ultimately lead you to your big idea. These objectives lie between your long-term goals and your daily tasks—they're like milestones on the path to achieving your vision. The objective is the next step you need to take to move closer to your three- or five-year goal. The sub-goals and sub-tasks are your implementation plan. If you follow these steps, meet these smaller objectives, you'll be well on your way to achieving the larger goal.

## Features of a Good Objective

A solid objective has several key features:

- It's achievable: You need to know that it can be done.

- It's written down: Put it in writing to make it real and keep everyone focused.

- It's specific: The more precise, the better.

- It's easy to understand: Especially for the people who will be doing the work.

- It provides focus: It keeps everyone aligned and on the same page.

- It's relevant: It needs to matter right now, in the current context of your operation.

- It's flexible: You should be able to adjust as needed without losing sight of the goal.

First and foremost, your objective needs to be achievable, and it has to be specific. Can you write it down in a single sentence? That simplicity will help keep your activities focused. It also needs to be relevant to what's happening right now and flexible enough to adapt if circumstances change. And most importantly, it must be understood by the people doing the work. Avoid flowery language—keep it simple and straightforward.

By setting clear, specific, and achievable objectives, and making sure everyone understands them, you'll be in a much better position to execute effectively and move your business toward its long-term goals.

When we're setting objectives, it's important to keep the SMART goals system in mind. That means our goals should be:

- Specific

- Measurable

- Attainable

- Relevant

- Time-bound

It's easy to get caught up in setting extremely lofty goals that might not be relevant to where you are right now. For example, if you're a brand-new franchise owner with dreams of owning five stores, each generating $5 million in sales, that's a fantastic long-term goal. But right now, with a newly opened business, that goal isn't immediately relevant. It's crucial to break it down into smaller, more manageable steps that are directly aligned with your current situation.

Think about it this way: your primary goal at the moment shouldn't be that big dream of owning multiple stores—it should be something that helps you get there. For example, you might focus on building a solid customer base or achieving a certain sales milestone in your first year. These are smaller, specific goals that are measurable and attainable given where you are right now. They're also directly relevant to your business's current needs and can be completed within a realistic timeframe.

Often, our objectives are stepping stones—smaller goals that lead us to the larger, more ambitious ones. Let's say you want to start offering a new service line, but right now, you need to ensure you have enough working capital to meet payroll every month. In this case, securing sufficient working capital becomes your immediate goal. It's specific, measurable, and relevant to your current situation, and it's an essential step toward that larger, future objective.

By focusing on these smaller, actionable goals, you can make meaningful progress that moves you closer to your big dreams. It's about making smart, strategic choices that align with where you are now, so you can build a solid foundation for future growth.

How do I know if an objective is good or bad?

Let's take an example from an automotive service center.

> *Montgomery Service Center will receive fewer customer complaints.*

Is this a good objective or a bad objective?

This is not a good objective. It is unclear how many are fewer. Can we measure fewer?

It can also be interpreted differently by different supervisors. The first thing you may hear is that this complaint or that complaint is not valid. Where are we measuring complaints? Are we using reviews or phone calls? How do we track those calls? Or do we look into every complaint or only specific types of complaints?

This objective is vague, not very specific, and not very measurable.

Now, let's examine a different business.

---

**_Midwest Hotel Group will achieve 80% room occupancy in the 3rd quarter of this year._**

---

Is this a good objective or a bad objective?

This is much better—clear and straightforward. Measuring room occupancy is a standard industry practice, so everyone knows exactly what we're trying to achieve. It's a measurable goal, which is key.

Let's say the hotel currently has a 60% room occupancy rate. Setting a goal to reach 80% occupancy in the next quarter could be both relevant and attainable for this location. It's a stretch, but within reach, and it's something the team can rally around.

But let's flip the scenario. If the hotel is only seeing a 10% room occupancy rate right now, aiming for 80% in just a few months might be a bit of a stretch—possibly even unrealistic. Sure, it's great to have ambitious goals, but it's also important to be realistic about what's achievable within the given timeframe.

The key here is to set goals that challenge you and your team but are still within the realm of possibility. It's about finding that sweet spot where your goals are ambitious enough to push you forward but realistic enough that you can actually hit them. When your goals are clear, measurable, and realistic, they give everyone something tangible to work toward—and that's when you start seeing real progress.

## So, how do you start setting objectives?

First things first, you have to be realistic. Sometimes, the resources you need just aren't available. If that's the case, your first objective might need to be securing those resources. Focus on what's truly important. Not all objectives are created equal—some will have a bigger impact on your business than others, so prioritizing is key. It's easy to get caught up in what's challenging or what seems like a quick win, but what's most essential is achieving the vision you've set for your business.

You've also got to be willing to ask the right questions. Start by getting crystal clear on what needs to be accomplished and who's going to do it.

Why is this objective relevant? Why does your business, or franchise, need to focus on this right now? Who's responsible for making it happen? And when do you expect to see results? It's important to think about whether the people responsible have the time, energy, and resources to get the job done. Do they have the skills and availability to achieve the objective? These are all questions you need answers to before moving forward.

We also need to remember to stay results-oriented. The whole point of setting objectives is to move the business forward—not to get bogged down in busyness. It's easy to get swept up in the day-to-day whirlwind, but if that happens, you risk creating obstacles that keep you from reaching your goals. That's why it's crucial to be clear with your goals and communication. Know exactly what needs to be done, why it's important, who's responsible, and always keep the end result in mind.

By being realistic, asking the right questions, and staying focused on results, you'll set objectives that truly drive your business forward.

**So, how do you define objectives?**

Well, objectives can take different forms depending on what you're trying to achieve. There are two main types: strategic and tactical. On top of that, there are six categories that objectives can fall into: qualitative, quantitative, decision-oriented, personal, creative, or routine. Let's break these down a bit.

---

## Two Types of Objectives

### Strategic

### Tactical

---

First, let's talk about the two types of objectives:

1. **Strategic Objectives:** These are the big-picture goals that usually involve things like costs, controls, budgets, profitability, and market decisions. Strategic objectives are all about the long-term game. They're focused on where you want to take your business in the future and often require more planning and foresight.

2. **Tactical Objectives:** On the other hand, tactical objectives are more about the here and now. They're usually short-term and focus on making routine tasks more efficient. These objectives are often part of a manager's day-to-day

responsibilities and help keep things running smoothly.

It's important to keep these two types in mind so you know whether you're dealing with something that requires a long-term strategy or a short-term task-related focus.

Objectives also fall into six categories.

---

## Six Categories of Objectives

Qualitative

Quantitative

Decision-Oriented

Routine

Creative

Personal

---

Objectives can be broken down into six main categories, each serving a different purpose in your business. Let's dive into what they are and how they play a role.

1. **Qualitative Objectives:** These are all about standards and quality, like aiming to provide "friendly service" or being "fast and dependable." The challenge with qualitative objectives is that they're often difficult to measure. How do you truly quantify something like friendliness or dependability?

It can be tough to pin down, but these objectives are still crucial because they shape the experience you offer to customers.

2. **Quantitative Objectives:** Unlike qualitative objectives, quantitative ones are much easier to measure. These typically relate to production achievements or numerical goals, such as the number of jobs completed or sales targets. If you're looking for something straightforward to track, quantitative objectives are where you'll want to focus.

3. **Decision-Oriented Objectives:** These come into play when you're facing a specific problem that needs to be solved, and the decisions you make will set the stage for other objectives. For instance, if your company vehicles are breaking down frequently, you might need to decide whether to buy or lease new ones. This decision will guide subsequent actions and objectives. It could also apply to bigger decisions, like whether to buy another franchise locally or expand into a new market.

4. **Routine Objectives:** Routine objectives are all about the day-to-day operations. These cover the repetitive tasks that keep your business running smoothly, like processing orders, delivery times, or how quickly you answer the phone.

While they might seem mundane, these objectives are essential for maintaining consistency and efficiency.

5. **Creative Objectives:** These are the goals that involve innovation and new ideas, often tied to marketing or business development. For example, you might set an objective to enhance brand recognition through a creative marketing campaign. Creative objectives are about applying fresh thinking to improve productivity and profitability.

6. **Personal Objectives:** These are the goals you set for yourself, whether they're related to your work or your personal life. For business owners, personal objectives often intersect with business goals. Maybe you want to take a six-week vacation in Italy—that's a personal objective. But to make that happen, you might need to grow your business or make specific changes, which creates a related business objective.

When you're setting objectives, it's helpful to think about which category they fall into. Are you aiming for something qualitative that enhances the customer experience? Are you focused on hitting a numerical target with a quantitative objective? Or are you making a key decision that will impact your future strategy? Understanding these categories helps you set well-rounded goals that address every aspect of your business.

Let's say you've selected your objective. It's specific, measurable, and you're ready to get moving. The next step is to bring in the right person or team to help you accomplish it. Here's where a lot of leaders stumble—they not only assign the goal but also dictate exactly how it should be achieved.

If you've hired the right people and they understand their role and your customer, they probably have more insight than you do into how to reach that goal. Your handpicked team knows the roadblocks you might not see and the issues you may not even be aware of. That's why it's so important to give them the autonomy to figure out the best path forward.

Dan Sullivan's "Who Not How" principle is a game-changer in this regard. Instead of getting caught up in figuring out how to do something, Sullivan suggests shifting the focus to who can help you achieve your goals. The idea is to leverage the talents, strengths, and expertise of others rather than trying to figure out every step on your own.

At its core, "Who Not How" is about collaboration and delegation. Instead of getting bogged down in the details of how to accomplish a task—something that can lead to feeling overwhelmed or stuck—ask yourself, "Who already knows how to do this? Who has the skills and experience to achieve this goal efficiently and effectively?" By identifying the right people, you can accelerate progress, lighten your workload, and often achieve better results than if you tried to do everything yourself.

This approach also fosters a mindset of growth and learning. When you collaborate with others who bring different skills and expertise to the table, it creates opportunities for mutual learning. Not only does this help you reach your current objectives more efficiently, but it also builds a network of relationships and resources that you can tap into for future projects. This is where some of your most valuable cross-training and professional development will happen.

Implementing the "Who Not How" principle involves recognizing the value others bring to the table, clearly communicating your objectives, and empowering the people tasked with the work. It's about creating a culture of trust where the focus is on achieving the outcome rather than micromanaging the process.

Ultimately, "Who Not How" helps build a more collaborative, innovative, and productive environment where everyone plays to their strengths and contributes to the collective success. When you select the right people to set the objectives and define the tasks, it makes all the difference in reaching your goals.

With the rise of digital marketing and online sales, I see a lot of businesses setting web-related objectives. A typical scenario might look like this: a business owner decides they want to increase online leads and sets a goal to "double the number of website visitors to 2,000 per month by December 31st." They then assign someone the task of writing two keyword-rich articles per week to help reach that goal.

At first glance, that might seem like a solid plan. But then someone suggests tweaking the objective to say, "We will increase customer visits from article postings by 25% in three months." That sounds even better, right? So, you bring in your web experts, and they start offering advice—writing two articles a week is great, but you also need to focus on search engine optimization (SEO). They recommend identifying meta tags, getting backlinks from other sites, and creating better internal links between your articles.

Now, you've got some solid advice from the web experts, and your plan is starting to shape up. But here's the thing: you still don't have all the right "Who's" in the room.

What if you had included your marketing manager, sales manager, or even a fractional Chief Marketing Officer (CMO) in the conversation from the start? They might have steered you toward a slightly different objective—one that's actually more aligned with what you truly want.

For example, instead of focusing on just getting more visitors, your objective could be: "We will increase conversions from web visitors by 20% in the next three months."

That's it! That's what you really need. It's not just about bringing more people to your website; it's about turning those visitors into customers. After all, having a ton of visitors doesn't do much good if they're not converting into sales. With this more refined objective, you'd see that the next steps should involve collaboration between your web team and your sales team. Suddenly, your focus shifts from simply driving traffic to optimizing conversions. And with that shift, your "Who's" have changed as well.

Now, instead of just pumping out articles, you might realize that videos, Google My Business optimization, or working with aggregators could be more effective for driving conversions. Your long-term vision becomes clearer, and your current objective is better aligned with that vision.

But this is where things can start to get complicated. How do you keep everyone on the same page and prevent them from feeling overwhelmed? This is where the concept of implementation sprints comes into play, and it's what we'll dive into next.

The key takeaway here is that it's not just about having an objective—it's about having the right objective, the right people involved, and a clear path to achieving it. By refining your goals and involving the right team members, you set yourself up for success and make sure every effort is moving you closer to your long-term vision.

# Chapter 12

---

# Implementation Sprints

"The path to success is to take massive, determined action."

Tony Robbins

A T ITS CORE, AN implementation plan is a roadmap that guides you toward achieving your Management by Objective (MBO) goals. It lays out the steps you need to take, who's responsible for each step, and when those steps should be completed. Think of it as the action blueprint that keeps everyone on the same path, making sure your team knows exactly where they're headed and how they'll get there.

In the day-to-day whirlwind of running a business, it's easy to get pulled in a million different directions, often away from your goals. That's why having a structured plan isn't just a nice-to-have—it's absolutely essential. Whether you're launching a new product, shifting your company's strategy, or refining your processes for better performance, a well-thought-out implementation plan is your secret weapon. It helps you steer through the complexities of change, manage potential risks, make the best use of your resources, and stay on track to reach your goals with clarity and precision.

In this chapter, we're going to break down the key components of an effective implementation plan. We'll start with the initial problem statement—where you define the root cause that's driving the need for action—and take you all the way to the final evaluation of your efforts. You'll learn how to set clear, actionable goals, measure your success, identify and address risks, and plan out tasks and resources efficiently.

But that's not all. We'll also dive into how to build the right team for the job, ensure everyone is accountable for their part, and manage your budget wisely. By the end of this chapter, you'll be equipped to create an implementation plan that doesn't just look good on paper but also delivers real, tangible results. Whether you're dealing with a major strategic shift or just trying to improve everyday operations, this plan will be your go-to guide for turning goals into reality.

## Understanding the Need for an Implementation Plan

Imagine you're about to set off on a road trip with a big group of friends, each driving their own car. You've all agreed on the destination, but how do you plan to get there if you don't have a map or GPS? Some people in your group like to take the scenic route, while others are all about getting there as fast as possible, even if it means driving through the night. You've got different vehicles, different speeds, and different preferences, but you want everyone to arrive together. What you need is a travel itinerary. This way, everyone knows the checkpoints—where to stop for gas, grab a meal, and eventually meet up at the hotel.

An implementation plan serves as the itinerary of your journey. It's your navigation system that keeps everyone on the same path, moving toward the same goal. It's not enough to know where you want to go; you also need to know the best way to get there, the stops you'll need to make along the way, and how to handle any detours. This section dives into why an implementation plan is so crucial—it's the tool that guides your project from start to finish, ensuring success along the way.

So, what exactly is an implementation plan? In simple terms, it's a detailed guide that outlines how you'll achieve a specific goal or objective within your business. It breaks down that big, ambitious goal into smaller, manageable pieces—laying out the tasks, timelines, roles, and resources needed to get the job done. Think of it as your team's playbook, spelling out each move so everyone knows what to do to win the game. It's all about turning strategy into actionable steps.

If you're dealing with a complex plan, this implementation plan is your go-to playbook!

Countless distractions can pull you off the critical path you've outlined in your grand vision. An implementation plan keeps you on track, allowing your business to stay agile and adapt without losing sight of what's important. It serves as the bridge between strategic planning and day-to-day operations, making sure that everything your team does aligns with your broader business goals.

When your implementation plan is in sync with your business strategy, it creates a powerful force that drives your company forward. It ensures that every department and team member isn't just busy but productive—actively contributing to the company's overall objectives. Being busy doesn't always mean you're effective. You can be swamped with tasks and still miss the mark if you're not focused on the right things. An implementation plan helps you align your efforts, prioritize what's most important, and make sure that your most critical goals don't get lost in the shuffle of daily operations.

This process of prioritization is key to maximizing efficiency, optimizing resource use, and making sure that, no matter how hectic things get, you're always moving toward your most important objectives. It's about working smarter, not just harder, and ensuring that every step you take is bringing you closer to your vision.

## Setting a Timeframe for Implementation

When it comes to setting a timeframe for your implementation plan, the timeline you choose can make or break its success. Many people start with annual goals, but here's the problem: a few months in, you might find that you've already achieved the goal because it wasn't ambitious enough, or worse, you've lost interest because the initial excitement has worn off. That's why shifting your focus from a traditional annual plan to a more agile, quarterly timeframe can be a game-changer for your project management approach.

### Why Quarterly Planning Works

Quarterly planning shines when it comes to agility. Time flies, and business conditions can change in the blink of an eye. What seemed like a top priority at the start of the year might not even be relevant a few months later. By setting a quarterly timeframe, you give your team the ability to respond quickly to these changes. This flexibility means you can pivot when needed, ensuring that your projects stay aligned with current business objectives, market trends, and customer needs.

### Avoiding Project Fatigue

Let's be honest—long-term projects that stretch over a year or more can wear your team down. The longer the timeline, the greater the risk of project fatigue setting in. When enthusiasm fades, productivity often takes a hit, and the quality of work can suffer. But when you break down those long-term projects into quarterly segments, you keep the work more manageable and keep your team's momentum and motivation high. This approach also allows for regular reassessment and realignment of goals and strategies, keeping the project fresh and engaging for everyone involved.

## The Power of Flexibility

One of the biggest advantages of a quarterly timeframe is the ability to pivot quickly. Flexibility is crucial in today's fast-paced business environment. With a quarterly approach, you're regularly reviewing progress, evaluating what's working (and what's not), and making adjustments as needed. This adaptability is key when you encounter unforeseen obstacles, stumble upon unexpected opportunities, or simply need to stay competitive in your market.

## Celebrate Wins More Often

Celebrating successes is essential for maintaining team morale and motivation. With quarterly implementation plans, you create more opportunities to mark milestones and recognize achievements. These celebrations are more than just a pat on the back—they reinforce the value of the team's hard work, build a positive work culture, and serve as motivation for the challenges ahead. By acknowledging accomplishments more frequently, you boost team spirit and confidence in the project's direction and leadership.

## How to Implement Quarterly Planning

To make the most of a quarterly planning approach, here are some steps to consider:

1. **Break Down Annual Goals into Quarterly Objectives:** Start by defining what you want to achieve over the year, then break these goals into smaller, more manageable quarterly milestones.

2. **Develop Flexible Strategies:** Design strategies that are adaptable, allowing you to shift direction quickly if needed.

3. **Set Regular Review Meetings:** Establish frequent check-ins at the end of each quarter to assess progress, discuss challenges, and adjust plans as necessary.

4. **Communicate Openly and Often:** Make sure all team members and stakeholders understand the quarterly focus and any changes to the plan. Keep everyone in the loop.

5. **Celebrate and Reset:** At the end of each quarter, take

the time to celebrate the wins before setting new goals and strategies for the next quarter.

## Why This Matters

Adopting a quarterly timeframe for your implementation plans offers a more dynamic, responsive, and sustainable approach to project management. If your team is just getting familiar with this process, you'll both appreciate the flexibility this timeline allows. For those used to annual plans, this shorter timeline not only improves project outcomes but also enhances team engagement and drives better overall results for your company.

In short, quarterly planning keeps your team focused, motivated, and adaptable, all while moving you closer to your long-term vision in manageable, actionable steps.

## Assembling the Right Team

The success of any project really comes down to the people who are working on it. Putting together the right team means more than just filling positions; it's about bringing together individuals who have the skills, experience, and attitudes needed to push the project forward. You're not just looking for warm bodies to fill seats—you're aiming to create a cohesive unit that works well together, with each member playing a vital role in the overall success.

Start by considering the specific tasks at hand and identifying the key competencies required to accomplish them. Then, find team members who not only possess those skills but are also genuinely committed to the project's goals. It's also worth noting that diversity within your team can be a huge asset. When you bring together people with different backgrounds, perspectives, and problem-solving approaches, you're more likely to come up with innovative solutions and richer outcomes.

Building a strong team isn't just about selecting the right people; it's also about creating an environment where they can thrive. This involves establishing clear roles and responsibilities, providing solid leadership and oversight, empowering your team members to take ownership of their tasks, and maintaining open lines of communication. When everyone knows what's expected of them and feels supported, you're setting the stage for success.

Accountability is a critical piece of the puzzle. It's what keeps the project moving forward and ensures that goals are met. Accountability begins with leadership. Every project needs a designated leader—a project manager or team lead—who's responsible for overseeing progress, ensuring the team stays aligned with the overall objectives, and being the go-to person when issues arise. This leader is the central point of contact and plays a crucial role in coordinating efforts, solving problems, and keeping the project on track.

But leadership doesn't stop there. The role of an executive sponsor is equally important. This person, typically a senior leader outside the immediate project team, provides the high-level support, resources, and guidance needed to navigate any organizational challenges that may come up. The executive sponsor is your advocate at the top level, helping to remove barriers and ensure that the project has what it needs to succeed.

By having both a hands-on project lead and an executive sponsor, you create a dual structure of accountability and support. This setup not only gives your project the leadership and resources it needs but also ensures that it has the authority and backing to overcome obstacles and reach its goals.

In short, assembling the right team is about more than just gathering skilled individuals—it's about creating a dynamic, supportive environment where everyone is aligned with the project's vision and feels empowered to contribute their best work. When you get this right, you set your project up for success from the very beginning.

## Defining Roles and Responsibilities

When it comes to teamwork, clear roles and responsibilities are absolutely essential. Without them, you risk confusion, missed deadlines, and a general sense of chaos. Each team member needs to know exactly what they're responsible for—what tasks they need to complete, what deliverables they're expected to produce, and when those deadlines are. This kind of clarity doesn't just prevent people from stepping on each other's toes; it ensures that every aspect of the project is covered and gives each person a sense of ownership over their part of the process.

One useful tool for defining roles and responsibilities is a responsibility assignment matrix, like a RACI chart. RACI stands for Responsible, Accountable, Consulted, and Informed. It's a simple framework that helps you map out who's doing what, who needs to sign off on decisions, who should be consulted for their input, and who just needs to be kept in the loop. It's a great way to streamline task delegation and make sure everyone knows exactly who to turn to for guidance or approval.

But let's talk about something that can really elevate your team's dynamics—choosing the right project leader. Instead of automatically assigning the highest-ranking person to lead, consider giving this opportunity to a mid-level team member. This approach has several benefits. First, it provides growth and leadership development for that mid-level employee. They get a chance to step up, take on more responsibility, and really shine. Second, it allows your senior managers to practice mentoring without adding more to their already heavy workload.

For example, imagine a scenario where your software development manager is leading a team that includes the VP of Marketing. This setup could be a game-changer for both individuals. The software development manager gets valuable leadership experience, while the VP of Marketing can provide crucial input to ensure the project meets their needs—without having to manage the day-to-day headaches of the project. It's a win-win situation that benefits everyone involved.

Now, if you find that all your VPs are hesitant to step back and let others lead, you might have a bigger issue on your hands. Their reluctance could be a sign that they're struggling with mentoring and building up their teams. If that's the case, it's worth addressing because part of being a great leader is knowing when to step back and let others grow.

In the end, defining roles and responsibilities is about more than just assigning tasks. It's about creating an environment where everyone knows their place, feels empowered to contribute, and has the opportunity to grow. When you get this right, you're not just setting your project up for success—you're building a stronger, more capable team for the future.

## Clear Objectives Align Stakeholders

In the last chapter, we dove into the importance of setting clear objectives. This principle is just as crucial in this next phase. Clear objectives are the foundation of any successful implementation plan. Everyone involved needs to understand these objectives and be fully committed to them. As you bring more people on board, the objectives might evolve slightly, but they should always remain SMART—Specific, Measurable, Achievable, Relevant, and Time-bound. It's essential that both the owner and the management team approve these objectives to ensure they align with your long-term vision and propel you toward your goals.

An implementation plan isn't just about moving from point A to point B; it's about making sure that every step taken by every part of your organization is synchronized, moving together as one cohesive unit toward the same destination. It's about creating harmony between your plan, your team, and your company's core objectives. This alignment ensures that even the smallest tasks contribute meaningfully to the bigger picture. In essence, it's about planning your work and then working your plan with a clear direction, strategic alignment, and a sharp focus on achieving tangible results.

### Define the Problem Statement

Before you jump into action, it's crucial to step back and ask, "Why are we doing this?" A well-defined problem statement is like the compass that sets the direction for your implementation plan. It's important to clearly articulate the issue you're addressing, why it needs to be tackled, and the impact of not solving it. Think of this problem statement as the rallying cry for your project—a unifying purpose that motivates your team to embark on this journey together.

## Deciding the Scope of Work

Once you've nailed down the problem, the next step is to outline the scope of work. This is where you define the boundaries of your project. What's included, and just as importantly, what's not? The scope of work serves as the project's blueprint, detailing the tasks that need to be completed, the processes that must be implemented, or the systems that need to be developed. It's your safeguard against scope creep, helping to keep your project focused and manageable. By clearly defining what success looks like, you give your team a target to aim for and a clear understanding of what's expected.

Let's take a real-world example: imagine your company's call center is transitioning to a new software system. Even if you're purchasing off-the-shelf software, the implementation might take more than just a few weeks. You'll need to answer a lot of questions. Will the new software integrate with or replace existing systems? How long will that integration take? What's the plan for minimizing downtime when switching from one system to another? Will your current hardware support the new software, or will you need upgrades? How does this new system interact with accounting? What about training—do you need custom training materials? Who's responsible for customization, if needed? Does your IT team know how to troubleshoot issues, or will you need a service contract?

Answering these questions is the essence of defining your project's scope. This process helps you identify who needs to be involved, what problems need solving, and how to keep the right teams focused on the right issues. You might find that you need separate scopes for different aspects, like technology setup and employee training, to ensure everything runs smoothly.

## Defining the End State Goal

Where do you want to be when all is said and done? Your end-state goal is the ultimate destination of your project's journey. It should be a clear, concise statement of what success looks like. This goal needs to be measurable so you can objectively determine whether you've achieved it. Whether it's increasing revenue by a certain percentage, reducing customer complaints, or successfully launching a new product, your end-state goal is the guiding star for all your project activities.

## Measuring Success: Setting the Criteria

Knowing when you've reached your destination is just as important as knowing where you're going in the first place. This is where setting clear criteria for success comes into play. Establish specific metrics or key performance indicators (KPIs) that will help you evaluate the project's outcomes. These metrics should align with your end-state goal and give your team a clear understanding of what success looks like in measurable terms. Whether it's tracking sales figures, customer satisfaction scores, or operational efficiency, these measurements will help you monitor progress and make informed decisions along the way.

For example, if your project aims to improve customer service, success could be measured by reducing the number of customer complaints or improving customer satisfaction scores. Setting these metrics upfront allows you to continuously assess the project's progress and make adjustments as needed, ensuring the project stays focused on achieving its key objectives. Plus, it gives you a way to celebrate milestones along the journey, keeping your team motivated and engaged.

## Identifying Risks and Planning Solutions

No journey is without its potential roadblocks, and your project is no different. Identifying possible risks early on allows you to prepare for them—or even prevent them altogether. This part of the plan should list the potential risks to your project, from resource constraints and technical challenges to stakeholder resistance. For each risk, propose possible solutions or mitigation strategies. Remember the concept of the premortem we discussed earlier? This is exactly where it comes into play. By thinking through potential failures in advance, you can steer clear of trouble before it derails your project.

Be sure to set aside resources for unexpected challenges, schedule regular review meetings to reassess risks, and establish contingency plans for critical project milestones. Incorporating risk management into your overall plan makes your project more resilient and better equipped to adapt to changes and overcome obstacles.

## Mapping the Journey with a Gantt Chart

When you're embarking on a project, visualizing the entire process can make a world of difference, and that's where a Gantt chart comes into play. Think of a Gantt chart as your project's roadmap—it visually lays out your project's schedule, showing you all the tasks that need to be completed, how long each will take, and how they all connect. It's like plotting your route on a map, helping you and your team understand not just the destination but every turn, pit stop, and overlap along the way.

A Gantt chart is particularly useful for keeping track of time and resources. It helps you see the sequence of activities at a glance, understand which tasks depend on others, and anticipate any potential roadblocks. For example, if you notice that a critical task falls right in the middle of someone's planned vacation or during a major holiday like Thanksgiving, you can adjust your schedule ahead of time to avoid delays. The Gantt chart becomes your guide to identifying the critical path—those tasks that absolutely must be completed on time to keep the entire project on track—and spotting potential delays before they become problems.

Creating a Gantt chart involves breaking down your big end goal into smaller, manageable tasks. It's like turning your ultimate objective into a series of high-level checkpoints that lead you step-by-step toward success. Each task gets assigned a timeline and a responsible person. For instance, your Gantt chart might include a task like "Create Training Program," with Sara in charge, assisted by Charles and Nate. While creating the training program involves many detailed steps, you don't need to list all those micro-tasks on the Gantt chart—that's Sara's responsibility to manage. The goal is to make the action plan clear enough that everyone on the team knows what needs to be done, when it needs to be done, and who's responsible for getting it done.

One of the best things about a Gantt chart is that it's not just a planning tool—it's also a tracking tool. As your project moves forward, you can update the Gantt chart to reflect your progress. This ongoing visual check-in helps you see how closely your project is sticking to the original timeline and lets you make adjustments as needed. If a task starts to fall behind schedule or if it looks like someone's workload is getting too heavy, the Gantt chart makes it easy to spot and fix the issue before it spirals out of control.

In essence, a Gantt chart is more than just a schedule; it's a dynamic tool that keeps your project on track, your team aligned, and your goals within reach. By using it to map out your journey, you can ensure that every step is accounted for, every delay is anticipated, and every team member is clear on their role in bringing the project to life.

## Incorporating Feedback Loops

Planning for success isn't just about setting goals and sticking to them; it's also about being flexible and open to feedback. Incorporating feedback loops into your project management process is crucial for continuous improvement. Whether the feedback comes from your team members, stakeholders, or customers, being receptive and willing to adapt ensures that your project stays on course and meets the needs of everyone it affects. Regular check-ins and retrospectives can be a vital part of this process, providing moments to reflect on what's working, what isn't, and how the plan can be adjusted for better outcomes.

To keep things running smoothly, the project owner should meet weekly with the primary project team leaders and the key person responsible for the project. These weekly check-ins can be short but effective, focusing on the progress of the Gantt chart deliverables and tackling any roadblocks that have popped up. Additionally, sending out weekly email updates and holding bi-weekly or monthly meetings with the owner and the broader management team is a great way to keep everyone in the loop. These meetings don't need to be long—just 5-10 minutes to quickly review progress and address any pressing issues.

This consistent communication process helps hold the team accountable for sticking to the timeline and ensures that everyone has the resources they need to succeed. It's also a great opportunity for coaching and mentoring, letting your team know that they have your support and encouragement. When people feel supported, they're more likely to stay motivated and focused on the tasks at hand.

Regular communication is the glue that keeps your project on track. Whether through team meetings, progress reports, or quick check-ins, these touchpoints offer valuable opportunities for updates, feedback, and course corrections. They foster transparency, help everyone see the progress being made, and ensure that the entire team remains aligned with the project's goals and timelines. This alignment is key to keeping momentum going and ultimately achieving the success you're aiming for.

## Financial Planning and Reporting

Once you've got a solid team and a clear action plan in place, it's time to turn your attention to the financial side of things. Effective financial planning and reporting are critical to ensuring that your project not only has the resources it needs to succeed but also keeps everyone in the loop about its financial health.

Every project, no matter how big or small, has to work within the limits of its financial resources. That's why establishing an approved budget right from the start is so important—it sets clear financial boundaries and expectations for everyone involved. This budget isn't just a rough estimate; it should be a detailed plan that accounts for all potential expenses, from labor and materials to technology and contingency funds for those unexpected costs that always seem to pop up.

One key point to remember is that labor costs aren't just about paying hourly wages. Even salaried employees have a cost associated with their time, especially when they're pulled away from their regular duties to focus on the project. By acknowledging this and making it clear that their time is a valuable resource, you're emphasizing the importance of the project over the usual day-to-day tasks. This shows your team that you understand the investment being made and that the project's success is a top priority.

But having a budget is only the first step. The real challenge lies in managing it effectively. This means keeping a close eye on spending, adjusting your financial forecasts as the project progresses, and making informed decisions to ensure that the project stays within its financial limits. Regular oversight is crucial here—typically handled by the project manager working closely with a financial controller or someone from the finance department.

To stay on top of things, your financial team should meet regularly to review financial reports, compare what was budgeted versus what's actually being spent, and make any necessary adjustments to keep the project on track. This ongoing process of monitoring and adjusting is essential for preventing cost overruns, ensuring that resources are used efficiently, and maintaining financial accountability throughout the project.

In short, effective financial planning and reporting are about more than just crunching numbers—they're about creating a strong foundation for your project, keeping it financially healthy, and making sure that everyone involved understands the importance of staying on budget. When done right, this approach not only helps to safeguard the project's success but also builds confidence among stakeholders that their investment is being well managed.

## Kickstarting the Implementation

With all the groundwork laid, a dedicated team assembled, and financial planning in place, it's time to shift from planning to action. This is the phase where your project starts to take shape in the real world. It's where all the strategizing, budgeting, and team-building efforts begin to pay off. Let's dive into what it takes to kickstart your implementation and manage your project day-to-day to ensure everything runs smoothly.

The start of your project is a pivotal moment—it's like the official green light that signals everyone to get moving. Often, this begins with a kick-off meeting, where the entire project team, key stakeholders, and possibly executive sponsors come together. This meeting isn't just a formality; it's your chance to ensure everyone is on the same page about the project's goals, timelines, and expectations. Think of it as gathering everyone at the starting line of a race—this is where you set the tone, address any lingering questions, and make sure everyone is ready to sprint toward the finish line. It's essential that everyone leaves this meeting with a clear understanding of their roles, the importance of their contributions, and how each piece of the puzzle fits into the bigger picture.

But getting the project off the ground is just the beginning. Keeping it on track and maintaining team momentum over time is a whole different challenge. Projects, especially long-term ones, can sometimes hit rough patches where progress slows, or the initial excitement starts to fade. As a project manager or team leader, it's your job to keep the team's spirits high and ensure the project continues to move forward. This is where celebrating milestones becomes key. Whether it's hitting a significant deadline, achieving a smaller goal, or even just acknowledging hard work, recognizing these moments can do wonders for team morale. Sometimes, all it takes is a reminder of why the project matters and how each person's role is crucial to its success to reignite that spark of motivation.

Execution and management are where your project truly comes to life. This phase isn't just about checking tasks off a list—it's about keeping the energy up, navigating the inevitable ups and downs with agility, and ensuring that every part of the project meets the high standards you've set. Starting strong with a well-organized and energetic kick-off, maintaining momentum throughout the project lifecycle, adapting to changes with flexibility, and consistently ensuring quality in every task are all critical to success.

This stage requires diligence, flexibility, and a deep commitment to seeing the project through to the end. But with the right approach, mindset, and leadership, you can steer your project to a successful completion, achieving your objectives and realizing the vision that you've worked so hard to bring to life.

## Evaluating Outcomes and Learning from Implementation

After all the hard work, planning, and dedication, your project has finally reached the finish line. But just because you've crossed that line doesn't mean the journey is over. This phase is about taking a step back to reflect on what you've achieved, evaluating how well your outcomes match up with your original goals, and extracting the valuable lessons that will guide you in future endeavors. Let's dive into how you can effectively wrap up your project and set the stage for ongoing improvement and success.

The first thing you'll want to do as you close out your project is to measure its success against the goals and criteria you set at the beginning. Remember those success metrics you outlined in your plan? Now's the time to revisit them and see how your results stack up. Did you hit your end-state goal? How do your outcomes compare to the benchmarks you set? Gathering data, feedback, and other forms of evidence is crucial during this process. It's important to approach this evaluation with an objective mindset—celebrate the wins, but also be honest about where the project may have fallen short. This step gives you a clear picture of the project's impact and effectiveness, helping you understand what worked and what didn't.

Next, you'll want to conduct a post-implementation review. Think of this as a debriefing session where you bring together the project team, stakeholders, and even customers or end-users to discuss the project in detail. What went well? What challenges did you face? How did the processes, teamwork, and resource allocation play out? This isn't about pointing fingers or assigning blame; it's about learning. By understanding the strengths and weaknesses of the project, you can gather insights that will be invaluable for future projects. Maybe there was a strategy that worked exceptionally well or a recurring issue that slowed progress. Identifying these patterns can help you replicate successes and avoid repeating mistakes.

One of the most valuable outcomes of this review process is the documentation of lessons learned. This isn't just a checklist of what went right or wrong—it's a detailed, honest, and actionable resource that can guide future projects. Whether it's a new best practice you've discovered, a risk factor that needs close monitoring, or feedback on a tool or methodology that worked well, these lessons are the legacy of your project. Make sure this document is easily accessible to other teams and consider sharing your findings across your organization. This way, your experiences can benefit not just your immediate team but the broader company as well.

In summary, evaluating outcomes and learning from your implementation is a crucial part of closing out any project. It's not just about looking back; it's about using that reflection to inform and improve future efforts. By carefully measuring success, conducting thorough reviews, and documenting your learnings, you create a foundation for continued growth and excellence in all your future projects.

## Recognizing Contributions and Celebrating Success

It's essential to take a moment to acknowledge the hard work and dedication that went into your project. Recognizing the contributions of your team and stakeholders isn't just a nice gesture—it's a powerful way to reinforce the value of everyone's efforts and boost morale. Whether the successes are big or small, celebrating them helps to close the project on a high note and leaves your team feeling appreciated and motivated for future challenges.

When you take the time to highlight individual and collective achievements, you're not only saying "thank you" but also setting the tone for what's important in your organization. Acknowledging the hard work, creativity, and perseverance that brought the project to life shows your team that their efforts matter and that their contributions are seen and valued. This kind of positive reinforcement can be a tremendous motivator, inspiring your team to bring the same level of dedication to the next project.

But recognizing success is just one part of the equation. The insights you've gained from evaluating your project's outcomes, conducting post-implementation reviews, and documenting lessons learned are invaluable tools for the future. Use these learnings as a springboard to accomplish even greater objectives down the road. Encourage a culture of continuous learning and adaptation, where every project—every sprint—builds on the last. This approach drives your organization toward greater efficiency, innovation, and success.

Evaluating outcomes and learning from implementation aren't just steps to check off at the end of a project—they're critical processes that complete the project lifecycle. These steps provide closure, offer insights for improvement, and allow you to celebrate both the journey and the achievements along the way. By systematically assessing performance, capturing lessons learned, recognizing efforts, and leveraging these insights for future projects, you create a culture of continuous learning and excellence. This not only enhances outcomes but also contributes to the ongoing growth and success of your team and your business.

It's easy for these plans to become part of the daily whirlwind, where the focus shifts away from the original objective. The process works and can have a dramatic impact on your business, but it's your responsibility to ensure that it stays true to the vision you set out to achieve. Don't let the objective morph into something that guarantees a successful project but falls short of driving the vision-driven outcomes you're aiming for.

To turn your vision into reality, keep your eyes on the outcomes while protecting and nurturing your culture. By doing so, you'll create an environment where your team can thrive, your projects can succeed, and your business can continue to grow in alignment with your long-term goals.

# Chapter 13

---

# Empowering Success with KPIs

"The path to success is to take massive, determined action, but without the right metrics, you'll never know if you're on track."

Tony Robbins

T HE ABILITY TO MEASURE, analyze, and act on key performance indicators (KPIs) is crucial for steering your business toward success. Think of KPIs as the pulse of your organization—measurable values that tell you how well you're doing in achieving your goals. They aren't just numbers on a spreadsheet; they represent your company's ambitions, reflect its operational efficiency, and serve as a guide for making informed decisions. By focusing on the right metrics, regularly tracking performance, and using data to fine-tune your approach, you can unlock your business's full potential and fast-track your journey toward your long-term vision.

KPIs empower your company by giving you clear, actionable insights into how things are going. They simplify complex data, turning it into information you can use to make precise, agile decisions. In a way, KPIs are like the headlights of your business, lighting up the path ahead so you can navigate confidently, even in uncertain conditions. They help foster a culture of continuous improvement and accountability by transforming abstract goals into concrete targets. When everyone in your organization understands and focuses on these targets, they align more naturally with the broader vision.

Selecting the right KPIs is like choosing the right tools for a job—they need to fit the task at hand and provide meaningful feedback on your progress. Regularly tracking and analyzing these metrics helps you pinpoint where things are working well and where there's room for improvement. This isn't just about measuring success; it's about driving productivity and ensuring that every action taken moves you closer to your vision, strategy, goals, and objectives. KPIs give you a clear, objective way to answer the critical question: "How are we really doing?"

By focusing on KPIs, you strip away the guesswork and emotional bias that can cloud judgment. Instead of relying on vague feelings like "I think we're doing okay," you get precise answers to how your day, week, or quarter really went. Did you hit your targets? Where did you fall short? This clarity is invaluable. It not only tells you where you stand but also guides you on where to go next. In this way, KPIs become one of the most powerful tools in your leadership toolkit, enabling you to lead with confidence, transparency, and a relentless focus on achieving your business aspirations.

How do we know that we are getting closer to reaching our interim and long-term goals?

"What gets measured gets managed."

Peter Drucker

KPIs are a big deal. They give us a clear picture of how things are going, allowing us to see if we're on track to meet our goals or if we need to make some adjustments. It's like keeping an eye on the scoreboard during a game—knowing the score helps us decide our next move.

Take fantasy football, for example. It has exploded in popularity, with more people glued to their fantasy apps, tracking their team's progress, than those actually watching NFL games on TV or streaming. Why is that? Because their fantasy score matters to them! People want to know if they're winning or losing, and if their team isn't performing well, they don't hesitate to make quick changes.

This natural tendency to monitor scores and take action is why choosing the right metrics is so important for your business. The right KPIs not only show you the score but also highlight your strengths and weaknesses, motivating you to make the necessary adjustments to improve. By measuring activity every day and focusing on metrics that truly reflect what's happening in your business, you're setting yourself up for success.

The phrase "Measure What Matters" became popular a few years ago, thanks to John Doerr's book of the same name. While his book dives deep into setting goals and measuring performance, I can sum it up in one sentence: We need to focus on the metrics that directly align with our business objectives. The KPIs we choose should guide and engage our team in what truly matters to the organization. They need to be in sync with our long-term vision and strategy.

For example, if your company's overall goal is growth and increasing capacity, but the main metrics you're measuring and rewarding are net profit, debt reduction, and cash holdings, then your team might focus on cutting costs and holding back on necessary investments instead of driving growth. The metrics you choose send a powerful message about what's important, so it's crucial to make sure they align with your long-term goals.

In this chapter, we'll dive into Key Performance Indicators and explore how data can boost your performance, engage your team, and help everyone improve individually. Let's start thinking about how the right metrics can transform your business.

## Leads vs. Lags: Understanding the Difference

When it comes to Key Performance Indicators (KPIs), understanding the difference between lead and lag indicators is crucial. Think of a lead indicator as a predictor—it's like getting a sneak peek at your future performance. If you can improve your lead indicators, you're setting yourself up for better long-term results. On the other hand, a lag indicator measures the final outcome. It's what tells you if your efforts have paid off.

To bring this to life, let's go back to our football analogy. Imagine you're analyzing a team's performance. A lead indicator might be the average yards gained per run. If that number is high, it's likely the team will get more first downs, leading to more scoring opportunities. Similarly, a higher completion rate in passing usually means more successful plays, which could ultimately result in a touchdown and a win.

### Applying Leads and Lags in Business

Now, let's shift this thinking to the business world. Imagine you're the Chief Marketing Officer (CMO) of a company, and you're trying to determine what metrics to focus on. You might consider five key categories:

1. **Attention:** The first thing you want to know is how much attention your business is getting. This could be measured by how many people see your ads on platforms like Facebook or YouTube. It could also be the number of cars driving past your storefront or the followers and subscribers you've accumulated on social media. Attention is your lead indicator—it shows potential interest.

2. **Leads:** Out of all that attention, how many people are taking the next step? Leads are those individuals who have expressed genuine interest—maybe they've clicked on your website link, called your business, or walked into your store. These are the people giving you a chance to make a sale.

3. **Conversion Rates:** This is where the rubber meets the road. Your conversion rate measures how many of those leads actually make a purchase. Picture this: every time someone walks into your store and you hear the bell on the door ring, that's a lead. But how many of those doorbell rings turn into sales? That's your conversion rate. Ideally, you want to see this rate improve over time, moving from, say, 10% to 15%, or even higher. Conversion rate is a key lag indicator that tells you how effective your sales process is.

4. **Dollars per Sale:** Also known as your average ticket or average invoice, this metric tells you how much each customer spends per transaction. There are many ways to increase this number—raising prices, cross-selling, upselling, bundling products, or offering volume discounts. The question to ask here is, "Are we making the most out of every sales opportunity?"

5. **Repeat Buyers:** Finally, how many of your customers are coming back for more? Repeat buyers are essential because they increase the Lifetime Customer Value (LCV). Acquiring a customer can be expensive, and you might even lose money on the first sale. But if that customer returns again and again, the cost of acquiring them is spread out over multiple transactions, turning that initial expense into a profit. For example, think about a restaurant. The first meal might just break even, but if the customer comes back several times, that's when you start seeing profits.

## The Power of Lifetime Customer Value

Let's dive a bit deeper into Lifetime Customer Value (LCV). It's a metric that helps you understand just how valuable a customer is over time. Take Walmart, for instance. Years ago, Walmart figured out that every person who walked through their doors, from a baby in a stroller to an adult, represented $250,000 in potential sales over their lifetime. If you knew that one customer could be worth $1,000 in sales in just their first year, how much would you be willing to invest to get them to choose your business? How would you treat them differently? How would you treat every phone call or question? Look back at your vision for you customers and your culture, does the KPI's you selected move you toward your vision and align with your culture?

## Putting It All Together

Understanding and measuring these lead and lag indicators in your business can help you make informed decisions that drive growth. By focusing on the right metrics—like attention, leads, conversion rates, dollars per sale, and repeat buyers—you'll have a clear picture of where your business is succeeding and where there's room for improvement. The goal is to use these insights to adapt, improve, and ultimately move closer to your long-term vision.

These are just a few examples from a marketing and sales perspective, but the beauty of KPIs is that they can be applied to every aspect of your business. If you're in production, you might focus on metrics like gross margin, units per hour, or billing per hour of labor. There's no shortage of KPI options that can help predict success and keep your business on track.

So, if you're thinking about introducing KPIs to your team for the first time, where do you start?

## Start Simple and Build From There

First things first: keep it simple. Pick a few straightforward KPIs that include both lead and lag indicators. Remember, this might be entirely new territory for your team, so start by setting a baseline. Can we measure these KPIs accurately? Are we consistent in how we measure them? Do we have a clear, written methodology and definition that everyone understands?

The key here is to ease your team into the process. Encourage them to view KPIs as tools for improvement, not as a means of assigning blame. Ask for their input—do they think these KPIs are relevant? Do they believe these metrics can forecast success? Most importantly, do they see opportunities for improvement?

## Set Attainable Goals

Once everyone is on the same page, it's time to set some goals. Start with something achievable, a quick win that you can celebrate as a team. This helps to build momentum and buy-in. For instance, if your current conversion rate is 10%, and the industry average is 80%, it's unrealistic to aim for that 80% right out of the gate. Instead, set an initial goal of, say, 15%. That's a 50% improvement—a significant step forward, yet attainable enough to build confidence and reinforce the value of KPIs.

When your team reaches that goal, make a big deal out of it. Celebrate the win. This positive reinforcement will help your team see KPIs as a path to success, not just another metric to track.

## Assess the Impact

The final step is to evaluate whether the lead indicators are influencing the lag indicators as expected. In other words, are the metrics you're tracking actually driving the results you want to see? For example, if your goal is to increase net profit, are the KPIs you're focusing on effectively boosting that bottom line? And importantly, are they doing so without negatively impacting other areas of the business?

It's crucial to understand how different metrics interact. For instance, you might find that focusing too heavily on short-term profitability could harm quality and customer experience. These numbers often move in opposite directions, so finding the right balance is key. This balance will ultimately shape your business culture and reputation in the marketplace.

## Creating a KPI-Driven Culture

Entire books and degrees are dedicated to mastering KPIs, but the basics we've covered can make a real difference in achieving your vision. Integrating these concepts into your daily business practices will create a culture focused on continuous improvement. Keep the focus on progress, avoid letting blame enter the conversation, and your business will be well on its way to flourishing.

KPIs are not just numbers on a spreadsheet—they're powerful tools that, when used correctly, can guide your business toward sustained success. By starting simple, setting achievable goals, and regularly assessing the impact, you'll be able to harness the full potential of KPIs to drive your business forward.

A few other KPIs you should consider which have helped me analyze a client's business. These KPIs should cover various areas, including marketing, operations, finance, and human resources.

## Top KPIs to Consider:

### Marketing:

- **Customer Acquisition Cost (CAC):** Measures the cost of acquiring a new customer.

- **Conversion Rate:** The percentage of visitors to your website or marketing campaign that converts into customers.

- **Customer Lifetime Value (CLV):** The total revenue a business can expect from a single customer account throughout their relationship.

- **Return on Marketing Investment (ROMI):** The profitability and effectiveness of marketing campaigns.

- **Lead Generation:** The number of new leads or potential customers generated.

## Operations:

- **Inventory Turnover:** Measures how quickly inventory is sold or used over a time period.

- **Operational Efficiency:** Ratios or metrics that indicate the efficiency of business operations, like cost per unit produced.

- **Quality Control:** Metrics related to product defects or returns rate.

- **Order Fulfillment Cycle Time:** The time from receiving an order to delivering the product or service.

- **Supply Chain Efficiency:** Time and cost metrics for sourcing materials and delivering products.

## Financial:

- **Gross Profit Margin:** The percentage of revenue that exceeds the cost of goods sold.

- **Net Profit Margin:** Indicates how much each revenue dollar translates into profit.

- **Return on Investment (ROI):** Measures the gain or loss generated on an investment relative to the money invested.

- **Cash Flow:** Monitoring the inflow and outflow of cash to understand the business's liquidity.

- **Debt-to-Equity Ratio:** Indicates the proportion of shareholders' equity and debt used to finance a company's assets.

## Human Resources:

- **Employee Turnover Rate:** The rate at which employees leave the organization and are replaced.

- **Employee Satisfaction:** Often measured through surveys to gauge the morale and engagement of the workforce.

- **Labor Cost Percentage:** The percentage of total operating costs that go towards paying employees.

- **Productivity Rate:** Measures output per employee or team to assess efficiency.

- **Training Return on Investment:** Evaluate the effectiveness of training programs in terms of improved performance and productivity.

It's crucial to remember that not all KPIs are created equal. The relevance and impact of each KPI can vary greatly depending on your specific business, industry, and where your company is in its growth journey. That's why it's so important to choose KPIs that align directly with your unique goals and objectives.

As we wrap up this chapter, it's clear that the real power of KPIs goes beyond just hitting short-term targets. They're about laying the groundwork for long-term success and staying competitive in a constantly changing market. KPIs are more than just numbers; they're tools that help you stay focused, track progress, and make informed decisions that drive your business forward.

By embracing KPIs, you're not just keeping up with the competition—you're setting the stage to thrive, innovate, and lead in your industry. KPIs have the potential to turn your vision into reality, translate strategies into tangible outcomes, and transform your efforts into real achievements. When you use them effectively, they become a powerful force that propels your business to new levels of success.

So, take the time to select the right KPIs for your business, and let them guide your journey. With the right KPIs in place, you'll not only achieve your goals but also build a solid foundation for a prosperous and sustainable future. Embrace the process, and watch as your business reaches new heights.

# Chapter 14

---

# Now is the Time to Turn Vision into Reality

> If you have the right people, doing the right things for the right reasons, headed in the right direction, they will make the right decisions at the right time to execute what you need to accomplish your strategy.
>
> Chris Moore

I T'S TIME TO TURN those big dreams into bold actions. This final chapter is your rallying cry—a call to step up and take decisive, game-changing moves to bring your vision to life.

You've spent time digging deep, reflecting on what truly matters, and crafting a vision that sparks excitement and purpose. You've imagined the future, felt the impact your company will have, and tasted the success waiting on the horizon. But now, it's time to move beyond imagining and start making it happen. It's time to step out of the planning phase and into the arena where your dreams meet reality.

Your vision is the guiding light that shapes every decision, every strategy, and every action. It's not just a lofty idea; it's a vivid, powerful picture of the future—one where your company has made a mark, changed lives, and achieved greatness. But remember, a vision without action is just a dream. It's time to bring that vision to life.

Start by taking a moment—no, take several moments—to deeply reflect on your core values. What drives you? What impact do you want your company to have on the world? Don't rush through this. Let these thoughts simmer. The clearer you are about your core values, the stronger and more resilient your vision will be.

Now, turn those dreams into a bold, straightforward vision narrative. This isn't the time to play small. Your vision should be daring, something that stretches you and your team. Make it so clear and specific that anyone who reads it can see exactly what you're aiming for. And most importantly, your vision should inspire. If it doesn't light a fire in you, your team, your customers, your vendors, and your community, then it needs to be bigger and more detailed. Everyone should see themselves in your vision and feel excited to be a part of it.

Close your eyes and picture your vision in vivid detail. What does success look like? What does it feel like? Imagine your company thriving, your customers raving, and your team feeling proud of the work they do. Picture the impact you're making, the growth your company is experiencing, and the legacy you're creating. This mental image is your compass—it will guide you through the tough times and keep you focused on your end goal.

Now, let's talk about your customers. They're the heart of your vision. Without them, your vision remains just a pipe dream. Knowing who your customers are and understanding their needs, desires, and challenges is crucial to shaping your strategy. Get to know your customers like the back of your hand. Who are they? What keeps them up at night? What do they crave that no one else is offering them?

Take your research and turn it into detailed customer personas. Give them names, faces, and stories. Understand their goals, pain points, and how your products or services can improve their lives. These personas aren't just for show—they're your guides as you develop your strategy and make decisions. The better you know your customers, the better you can serve them.

But don't stop at creating personas. Engage with your customers regularly and truly listen to what they have to say. Ask them questions, pay attention to their feedback, and adjust your approach accordingly. Use social media, surveys, and direct interactions to stay connected. The more you listen, the more attuned you'll be to their needs, and the more loyal they'll become.

A vision without a strategy is just a dream. Your strategy is the blueprint that outlines the steps needed to achieve your vision and reach your ideal customer. Start by setting clear, measurable objectives and action plans. Align them with your vision, and make sure they're ambitious enough to push you forward but realistic enough to be within reach.

Your team is the engine that drives your vision forward. Building the right culture and equipping your team with the skills and attributes needed for success are critical. When hiring, look for people who not only have the skills you need but also share your values and commitment to the vision. Skills can be taught, but alignment with your vision is something deeper. You want individuals who bring positive energy, creativity, and a willingness to go the extra mile.

Your vision should be at the core of your company culture. It should be what everyone rallies around—the reason they come to work every day. Embed it into every aspect of your culture, from how you communicate to how you reward performance. When your team is aligned with your vision, they become an unstoppable force.

Invest in training and development programs that enhance your team's skills and prepare them to execute your strategy and serve your customers. This isn't just about technical skills; it's about building a team that's resilient, adaptable, and ready to tackle any challenge that comes their way.

Now is the time for action—relentless, focused action. It's what bridges the gap between vision and reality. It's about taking bold steps, making tough decisions, and staying committed even when the going gets tough. Implement your strategy with precision and urgency. Don't wait for the perfect moment—it doesn't exist. Start now, monitor your progress, make adjustments as needed, and keep moving forward. Execution is everything.

Challenges and setbacks will come. But here's the thing—setbacks aren't failures; they're learning opportunities. Stay resilient, learn from your mistakes, and keep your eyes on the vision. Remember, the journey is just as important as the destination. Celebrate the milestones along the way. Recognize your team's hard work, acknowledge the small victories, and use these moments to build momentum. Celebrating isn't just about recognizing success; it's about fueling the energy to keep going.

You have the vision, the plan, and the tenacity to see it through. This is your moment. Embrace it with passion and determination.

Now is the time to act. Seize this moment with everything you've got. Lead with conviction, inspire with your vision, and take the decisive steps needed to turn your dreams into reality. The world is waiting for your impact, and the future is yours to shape.

Rise up, take action, and make your vision a reality.

Your real journey starts now.

# Acknowledgements

There are so many people to thank. Dad taught me what it meant to be a real man, and what faith in action really means. My mom was the one who first taught me to love books, and how to live with joy. My first-grade teacher, Mrs. Patsy Spikes, taught me to read and to enjoy learning. I'm thankful for my college mentors, Lowell Sturgill and Bert Tippett. Your impact on my life will never be forgotten.

No one gets anywhere on their own. I am thankful for the team members who suffered as I learned and those who picked me up and carried me along the way. I am grateful for those business owners who shared what was working and what was not. We learned from each other, and our legacies will forever be intertwined.

I also want to thank those who have encouraged me over the last few years to step out and share my message with a broader audience. John Maxwell, Jane Atkinson, Jen McDonough, Jeff Goins, Erick Rheam, and Rick Clemons. You each stepped into my life at different times and changed me for the better.

# About the Author

Chris Moore is a sought-after speaker, bestselling author, and business consultant with over 25 years of experience helping individuals and organizations transform their vision into reality. With a passion for leadership and a knack for amplifying communication, Chris has guided countless teams to achieve breakthrough results through his dynamic keynotes, workshops, and consulting services.

Chris's unique approach to leadership combines practical strategies with deep insights into human connection, allowing him to engage and inspire audiences from the moment he steps on stage. His ability to connect with people and provide actionable tools has made him a favorite among business leaders and entrepreneurs looking to elevate their teams and drive performance.

When he's not on the road speaking or working with clients, Chris enjoys traveling and creating lasting memories with his wife, Melissa, and their son, Bryson. An avid guitarist, Chris also finds time to unwind by playing one of his many guitars.

Learn more about Chris and his work at ChrisMooreLive.com and MaximumImpactEnterprises.com.

# Keynotes

Invite Chris Moore to your organization for an inspiring, dynamic keynote or workshop With over 20 years of experience leading through challenging times, Chris brings a wealth of knowledge and a unique perspective on leadership, growth, and performance. His presentations are customized, interactive, and focused on practical outcomes like leadership development, team engagement, and performance enhancement. Perfect for business leaders and visionary changemakers, Chris's approach bridges daily operations with overarching goals.

For an event that motivates and provides tangible strategies for improvement, reach out to Chris. Your team will benefit from his insights on casting vision, building trust, increasing engagement, and driving performance. To book Chris for your next event or company meeting, email chris@chrismoorelive.com. Transform your organization's vision into reality with Chris Moore's engaging and impactful keynote.

For more detailed information about Chris Moore's offerings and his approach, you can visit ChrisMooreLive.com.

# www.ChrisMooreLive.com

▶ @chrismoorelive

in @chrismoorelive

X @chrismoorelive

f @chrismoorelive

○ @chrismoorelive

♪ @chrismoorelive

# Can You Do Me a Favor?

Did you get value from this book?

My hope is that you did. It's easy to dream but much more challenging to turn it into reality. This book can help those who were as frustrated and beaten down as I was.

If you enjoy the book, I'd love to ask you for a favor. Please share this with at least one person who could benefit from these principles and strategies.

My goal is to help 10,000 people Turn Vision into Reality. It's not an easy task. I need your help to do it.

Your support makes a huge difference in making that happen.

Lastly, I would love to hear from you anytime about your progress. You can email me at chris@chrismoorelive.com

Thanks in advance for your help!

I look forward to hearing from you.